Satchmo

My Life in New Orleans

Satchmo

My Life in New Orleans

by LOUIS ARMSTRONG

New introduction by

DAN MORGENSTERN

A DACAPO PAPERBACK

Library of Congress Cataloging in Publication Data

Armstrong, Louis, 1900-1971.
  Satchmo: my life in New Orleans.

  (A Da Capo paperback)
  Reprint. Originally published: New York: Prentice-
Hall, 1954. With new introd.
    1. Armstrong, Louis, 1900-1971 — Childhood and youth.
  2. Jazz musicians — United States — Biography. 3. Jazz.
  music — Louisiana — New Orleans. 4. New Orleans. (La.) —
  History. I. Title.
  ML419.A75A3   1986   785.42′092′ [B]   86-13592
  ISBN 0-306-80276-7

This Da Capo Press paperback edition of *Satchmo: My Life in New Orleans*
is an unabridged republication of the edition published in New York in
1954, here supplemented with a new introduction by Dan Morgenstern.
It is reprinted by arrangement with Prentice-Hall, Inc.

Published by Da Capo Press, Inc.
A Subsidiary of Plenum Publishing Corporation
233 Spring Street
New York, N.Y. 10013

INTRODUCTION TO THE
DA CAPO EDITION

"EVER SINCE I WAS a small kid," writes Louis Armstrong in these memoirs, "I have always been a great
observer." Indeed, it is a vivid picture Armstrong
draws for us of life as he experienced and witnessed it
during the first two decades of this century in New
Orleans.

By contemporary Western standards, this life was
one of deprivation and extreme poverty, but the tone of
Satchmo is far removed from, say, Orwell's *Down and Out
In Paris and London*. But then, Armstrong was not an
educated man, and there was no distance between him
and those with whom he shared his early lot in life. He
was different from most of them, and the key difference

[v]

was character. While he doesn't pass judgment on the "gamblers, hustlers, cheap pimps, thieves (and) prostitutes" among whom he was raised, it is clear throughout this book that his values, from a very early age on, differ from theirs.

This is perhaps most poignantly revealed in a passage toward the end of the narrative. Armstrong has just returned home from a six-month stint on the Mississippi steamer *St. Paul,* with more money in his pockets than ever before. He heads straight for the old neighborhood, and the first familiar face he encounters is that of Black Benny. This hustler and gifted part-time drummer is one of the most strongly-drawn figures in *Satchmo,* an older man of great physical strength and real courage who early on becomes one of "Little Louis'" many protectors, and whom the youngster clearly admires.

Benny is happy to see his young protégé again, but immediately makes him aware that he knows about the money:

> He asked me to stand him a drink, and who was I to refuse the great Black Benny. . . . Nobody else ever did. When the drinks came I noticed that everybody had ordered. I threw down a twenty dollar bill to pay for the round which cost about six or seven bucks. When the bartender counted out my change Black Benny immediately reached for it saying, "I'll take it." I smiled all over my face. What else could I do? Benny wanted the money and that was that. Besides I was so fond of Benny it did not matter anyway. I do believe,

[vi]

however, if he had not strongarmed that money out of me I would have given him lots more. I had been thinking about it on the train coming home....But since Benny did it the hard way I gave the idea up. I sort of felt he should have treated me like a man, and I did not like the way he cut under me....So I disgustedly waited for an opening to leave, and did.

Though Armstrong doesn't comment further, one senses that this experience, almost as much as his new-found confidence in his own musical abilities and his growing estrangement from his wife, is his "opening to leave" his hometown and his old environment for good. Armstrong was not immodest in his claim to be a great observer of human nature.

Armstrong credits his maternal grandmother, who raised him to the age of five, and his mother, to whom he was deeply attached, with instilling in him the system of values that would carry him through his extraordinary life and enable him to confront with serenity experiences and situations he could not have imagined in his wildest childhood dreams. As he describes them, these values seem deceptively simple:

"...I didn't go any further than fifth grade in school myself. But with my good sense and mother-wit, and knowing how to treat and respect the feelings of other people, that's all I've needed through life."

And, in a variation on the same basic theme (variations, after all, are of interest in the work of a great improvising artist): "I managed to teach him (his adopted son, Clarence, a second cousin) the necessary things in life, such as being courteous, having respect for other people, and last but not least, having good common sense."

How does a man who didn't finish fifth grade come to write a book? Before we attempt to answer that question, we must deal briefly with the doubts that have been cast on the authorship of *Satchmo* by James Lincoln Collier in *Louis Armstrong: An American Genius,* which does not fulfill the promise of its title. Lumping together two very different books—the one to hand and the 1936 *Swing That Music*—Collier states: "The two books Armstrong signed—one of which he probably wrote, in the main—are unreliable." The attack on Armstrong's veracity is unworthy, while "probably" and "in the main" can be easily disposed of. A copy of the typescript of *Satchmo* the (author's working title was *The Armstrong Story*) resides in the archives of the Institute of Jazz Studies at Rutgers University, and I have carefully compared it to the published text. Though substantial editing was done, it was mostly a matter of changing Armstrong's three-dot style to conventionally punctuated sentence-structure. The words are essentially Armstrong's own, and nothing of importance he did not write has been put in his mouth. Anyone at all familiar with the editing process as applied to many famous works of fiction, not to mention non-professional autobiographies, should consider Collier's qualifying "in the main" wholly irrelevant. (If anything, the original version reads better.)

[viii]

As for Collier's "probably," only Armstrong could have typed that manuscript. His approach to language, spelling, and syntax—even his touch on the typewriter—is inimitable, and as distinctive as his handwriting. The authenticity of *Satchmo* is not in question. (*Swing That Music* is heavily ghosted and in any event as much—or more—a paean to Swing and an attempted introduction to its musical methods as an autobiography. Yet it has the distinction of being the first book published about a jazz musician, unless Paul Whiteman and Vincent Lopez fit that description.)

How, then, did this "uneducated" and "deprived" man come to be a writer, and a real one, with a clear and distinctive voice of his own? We know that Armstrong already owned a typewriter and knew how to use it when he first arrived in Chicago to join King Oliver's band—the climactic event in *Satchmo*. The earliest surviving typed letter by Armstrong I've seen is dated Sept. 1, 1922, and it contains complaints that three previous letters (one to the recipient, two to other friends) have gone unanswered. Armstrong left New Orleans on Aug. 8, so we can conclude that he was already a fairly prolific correspondent. Some 20 years later, he was capable of tossing off a 13-page single-spaced missive, though most of his known letters average a page or two. (Short greetings and strictly personal messages were always handwritten, preferably in green ink, but the Institute's archives also contain a biographical sketch of some 10,000 words penned in this manner, dating from 1944. It was written "on the road," probably while the typewriter was packed away. Incidentally, insofar as its subject matter overlaps with *Satchmo*'s the facts are consistent.)

Clearly, Louis Armstrong loved to write, and, given stylistic and linguistic idosyncrasies, he wrote exceptionally well. Writing was a natural extension of his gift for the spoken word, his love of story-telling, and his ceaseless fascination with the foibles of human beings. Graceful, effortless, unselfconscious, but always at pains to make his meaning clear (the *Satchmo* manuscript contains many parenthetical explanations to the potential uninitiated reader), Armstrong's prose style reflects structural and emotional aspects of his musical expression. It is, of course, much more down to earth, but after all, Armstrong wrote for relaxation. Music, as even a superficial reading of this book reveals, was work.

The work ethic was fundamental to Armstrong's outlook on life. In this respect, he was most certainly a moralist, though his tolerance for a broad range of behavior was vast. His sense of humor combined with this tolerance prevents him from striking a self-righteous pose, as a writer and a man. Nothing human was alien to him, yet the standards he applied to his own behavior were quite strict, from an ethical standpoint. Collier, ever the puritan, finds Armstrong's fondness for eating "obsessive," yet Armstrong explains succinctly in these pages why he is against self-deprivation. A fellow musician aboard the *St. Paul* nearly starves himself in order to invest all his earning

[x]

in cotton farming. But the boll weevils devour his cotton, and he almost becomes suicidal. "I'll never be rich," Armstrong concludes from observing this nasty trait, "but I'll be a fat man." He did become rich, of course, but never spent much on himself. He wives were well provided for, but he saw no need for "a flock of suits." And, perhaps because he never forgot the generosity his early playing had inspired from his "deprived" audiences of whores, pimps, and hustlers, he gave away all he could afford as long as he lived.

The music always came first, but even in this Armstrong has often been misunderstood. Why, it has been asked, did he leave the direction of his bands, especially the big ones from 1929 to 1947, mainly to other (and, needless to say, lesser) musicians? The question is answered perfectly well in these pages:

"I never cared to become a band leader; there was too much quarreling over petty money matters. I just wanted to blow my horn peacefully as I am doing now. I have always noticed that the band leader not only had to satisfy the crowd but that he also had to worry about the box office." Armstrong let others count the house and mind the payroll; he had more important things to do, such as making music. Others (Duke Ellington for one) found more ingenious and sophisticated ways of confronting this dilemma, but Armstrong knew that when he picked up his horn, or opened his mouth to sing, the relative quality of the accompaniment became strictly a secondary concern.

Many other themes struck up in this book are

recurrent in Armstrong's comments, written or spoken, about his music. There was his love and respect for King Oliver (his mentor and first and lasting idol) above all, and then for all the music and musicians he'd grown up with. Though he would go far beyond what they had accomplished, to him they remained the best of all time. Was this nostalgia? Perhaps; this book makes it evident that while Armstrong quickly outgrew his native environment, he retained a strong empathy for it all his life. But it was more than simply that, or even the displeasure with newer trends in jazz that had become apparent in his attitude by the time he began to write *Satchmo*. It was, I think, the feeling and the originality that the musicians he admired in his youth brought to their art and craft. It was truly new, and they had made it up; nothing like it had been heard before. And even as he went on to create what seems to us far more remarkable and adventurous music (from which what he later came to disdain so clearly sprang), he remained a traditionalist at heart, a man who played and sang pretty or funny songs to make people feel pleasure.

Today, we say that Louis Armstrong saw himself as an "entertainer," and understand this term to mean something less than "artist." Paradoxically, what Armstrong created to entertain happens to surpass in artistry a great deal (if not most) of what self-styled artists have to offer. This paradox never interested or concerned Armstrong himself. He did what he did; he was who he was. And what he did and was eludes analysis and explanation. Reading this little book without preconceptions, and above all without the blinding burden of modernistic sociological and psychological notions about class, race, "intellect," and high versus popular culture, will bring you a bit closer to the mysterious wellsprings of Louis Armstrong's art, and to one of nature's noblemen — in the truest sense of the poet's term.

— DAN MORGENSTERN
New York City
May, 1986

Errata: The names of musicians are frequently misspelled in the text. Thus, Ducson should be *Duson,* Gasper-*Gaspar,* Harry Zeno - *Henry* Zeno, Powlow-*Paolo,* Fields-*Filhé,* Mauret-*Moret,* Dewey-*Duhé,* Backet-*Bacquet.* As for Bacquet, no matter how his last name is rendered, he was indisputably a clarinetist, and it is an E-flat *clarinet,* not cornet, which he played in the Excelsior Brass Band. Kid Ory's hometown is *Laplace,* not La Blast, and it was the *Edelweiss,* not Idlewise Gardens in Chicago. "Stock ties" seems to be a mishearing of Ascot ties.

chapter 1

WHEN I WAS BORN in 1900 my father, Willie Armstrong, and my mother, May Ann — or Mayann as she was called — were living on a little street called James Alley. Only one block long, James Alley is located in the crowded section of New Orleans known as Back o' Town. It is one of the four great sections into which the city is divided. The others are Uptown, Downtown and Front o' Town, and each of these quarters has its own little traits.

James Alley — not Jane Alley as some people call it — lies in the very heart of what is called The Battlefield because the toughest characters in town used to live there, and would shoot and fight so much. In that one block between Gravier and Perdido Streets more people were crowded than you ever saw in your life. There were churchpeople, gamblers, hustlers, cheap pimps, thieves, prostitutes and lots of children. There were bars, honky-tonks and saloons, and lots of women walking the streets for tricks to take to their "pads," as they called their rooms.

Mayann told me that the night I was born there was a great big shooting scrape in the Alley and the two guys killed each other. It was the Fourth of July, a big holiday in New Orleans, when almost anything can happen. Pretty near everybody celebrates with pistols, shot guns, or any other weapon that's handy.

When I was born my mother and father lived with my grandmother, Mrs. Josephine Armstrong (bless her heart!), but they did not stay with her long. They used to quarrel something awful, and finally the blow came. My mother moved away, leaving me with grandma. My father went in another direction to live with another woman. My mother went to a place at Liberty and Perdido Streets in a neighborhood filled with cheap prostitutes who did not make as much money for their time as the whores in Storyville, the famous red-light district. Whether my mother did any hustling, I cannot say. If she did, she certainly kept it out of my sight. One thing is certain: everybody from the churchfolks to the lowest roughneck treated her with the greatest respect. She was glad to say hello to everybody and she always held her head up. She never envied anybody. I guess I must have inherited this trait from Mayann.

When I was a year old my father went to work in a turpentine factory out by James Alley, where he stayed till he died in 1933. He stayed there so long he almost became a part of the place, and he could hire and fire the colored guys who worked under him. From the time my parents separated I did not see my father again until I had grown to a pretty good size, and I did not see Mayann for a long time either.

Grandmother sent me to school and she took in washing and ironing. When I helped her deliver the clothes to the white folks she would give me a nickel. Gee, I thought I was rich! Days I did not have to go to school grandmother took me with her when she had to do washing and housework for one of the white folks. While she was working I used to play games with the little white boys out in the yard. Hide-and-go-seek was one of the games we used to play, and every time we played I was It. And every time I would hide those clever little white kids always found me. That sure would get my goat. Even when I was at home or in kindergarten getting my lessons I kept wishing grandma would hurry up and go back to her washing job so I could find a place to hide where they could not find me.

One real hot summer day those little white kids and myself were having the time of our lives playing hide-and-go-seek. And of course I was It. I kept wondering and figuring where, oh where was I going to

[9]

hide. Finally I looked at grandma who was leaning over a wash tub working like mad. The placket in the back of her Mother Hubbard skirt was flopping wide open. That gave me the idea. I made a mad dash over to her and got up under her dress before the kids could find out where I had gone. For a long time I heard those kids running around and saying "where did he go?" Just as they were about to give up the search I stuck my head out of grandma's placket and went "P-f-f-f-f-f! "

"Oh, there you are. We've found you," they shouted.

"No siree," I said. "You wouldn't of found me if I had not stuck my head out."

Ever since I was a baby I have had great love for my grandmother. She spent the best of her days raising me, and teaching me right from wrong. Whenever I did something she thought I ought to get a whipping for, she sent me out to get a switch from the big old Chinaball tree in her yard.

"You have been a bad boy," she would say. "I am going to give you a good licking."

With tears in my eyes I would go to the tree and return with the smallest switch I could find. Generally she would laugh and let me off. However, when she was really angry she would give me a whipping for everything wrong I had done for weeks. Mayann must have adopted this system, for when I lived with her later on she would swing on me just the same way grandmother did.

I remember my great-grandmother real well too. She lived to be more than ninety. From her I must have inherited my energy. Now at fifty-four I feel like a young man just out of school and eager to go out in the world to really live my life with my horn.

In those days, of course, I did not know a horn from a comb. I was going to church regularly for both grandma and my great-grandmother were Christian women, and between them they kept me in school, church and Sunday school. In church and Sunday school I did a whole lot of singing. That, I guess, is how I acquired my singing tactics.

I took part in everything that happened at school. Both the children and the teachers liked me, but I never wanted to be a teacher's pet. However, even when I was very young I was conscientious about everything I did. At church my heart went into every hymn I sang. I am still a great believer and I go to church whenever I get the chance.

After two years my father quit the woman he was living with, and went back to Mayann. The result was my sister Beatrice, who was later nicknamed "Mama Lucy." I was still with my grandmother when she was born, and I did not see her until I was five years old.

One summer there was a terrible drought. It had not rained for months, and there was not a drop of water to be found. In those days big cisterns were kept in the yards to catch rain water. When the cisterns were filled with water it was easy to get all the water that was needed. But this time the cisterns were empty, and everybody on James Alley was frantic as the dickens. The House of Detention stables on the corner of James Alley and Gravier Street saved the day. There was water at the stable, and the drivers let us bring empty beer barrels and fill them up.

In front of the stables was the House of Detention itself, occupying a whole square block. There prisoners were sent with "thirty days to six months." The prisoners were used to clean the public markets all over the city, and they were taken to and from their work in large wagons. Those who worked in the markets had their sentences reduced from thirty days to nineteen. In those days New Orleans had fine big horses to pull the patrol wagons and the Black Maria. I used to look at those horses and wish I could ride on one some day. And finally I did. Gee, was I thrilled!

One day when I was getting water along with the rest of the neighbors on James Alley an elderly lady who was a friend of Mayann's came to my grandmother's to tell her that Mayann was very sick and that she and my dad had broken up again. My mother did not know where dad was or if he was coming back. She had been left alone with her baby — my sister Beatrice (or Mama Lucy) — with no one to take care of her. The woman asked grandmother if she would let me go to Mayann and help out. Being the grand person she was, grandma consented right away to let me go to my mother's bedside. With tears in her eyes she started to put my little clothes on me.

"I really hate to let you out of my sight," she said. "I am so used to having you now."

"I am sorry to leave you, too, granny," I answered with a lump in my throat. "But I will come back soon, I hope. I love you so much, grandma. You have been so kind and so nice to me, taught me everything I know: how to take care of myself, how to wash myself and brush my teeth, put my clothes away, mind the older folks."

She patted me on the back, wiped her eyes and then wiped mine. Then she kind of nudged me very gently toward the door to say good-bye. She did not know when I would be back. I didn't either. But my mother was sick, and she felt I should go to her side.

The woman took me by the hand and slowly led me away. When we were in the street I suddenly broke into tears. As long as we were in James Alley I could see Grandma Josephine waving good-bye to me. We turned the corner to catch the Tulane Avenue trolley, just in front of the House of Detention. I stood there sniffling, when all of a sudden the woman turned me round to see the huge building.

"Listen here, Louis," she said. "If you don't stop crying at once I will put you in that prison. That's where they keep bad men and women. You don't want to go there, do you?"

"Oh, no, lady."

Seeing how big this place was I said to myself: "Maybe I had better stop crying. After all I don't know this woman and she is liable to do what she said. You never know."

I stopped crying at once. The trolley came and we got on.

It was my first experience with Jim Crow. I was just five, and I had never ridden on a street car before. Since I was the first to get on, I walked right up to the front of the car without noticing the signs on the backs of the seats on both sides, which read: FOR COLORED PASSENGERS ONLY. Thinking the woman was following me, I sat down in one of the front seats. However, she did not join me, and when I turned to see what had happened, there was no lady. Looking all the way to the back of the car, I saw her waving to me frantically.

"Come here, boy," she cried. "Sit where you belong."

I thought she was kidding me so I stayed where I was, sort of acting cute. What did I care where she sat? Shucks, that woman came up to me and jerked me out of the seat. Quick as a flash she dragged me to the back of the car and pushed me into one of the rear seats. Then I saw the signs on the backs of the seats saying: FOR COLORED PASSENGERS ONLY.

"What do those signs say?" I asked.

"Don't ask so many questions! Shut your mouth, you little fool."

There is something funny about those signs on the street cars in New Orleans. We colored folks used to get real kicks out of them when we got on a car at the picnic grounds or at Canal Street on a Sunday evening when we outnumbered the white folks. Automatically we took the whole car over, sitting as far up front as we wanted to. It felt good to sit up there once in a while. We felt a little more important than usual. I can't explain why exactly, but maybe it was because we weren't supposed to be up there.

When the car stopped at the corner of Tulane and Liberty Streets the woman said:

"All right, Louis. This is where we get off."

As we got off the car I looked straight down Liberty Street. Crowds of people were moving up and down as far as my eyes could see. It reminded me of James Alley, I thought, and if it weren't for grandma I would not miss the Alley much. However, I kept these thoughts to myself as we walked the two blocks to the house where Mayann was living. In a single room in a back courtyard she had to cook, wash, iron and take care of my baby sister. My first impression was so vivid that I remember it as if it was yesterday. I did not know what to think. All I knew was that I was with mama and that I loved her as much as grandma. My poor mother lay there before my eyes, very, very sick . . .

Oh God, a very funny feeling came over me and I felt like I wanted to cry again.

"So you did come to see your mother?" she said.

"Yes, mama."

"I was afraid grandma wouldn't let you. After all I realize I have not done what I should by you. But, son, mama will make it up. If it weren't for that no-good father of yours things would have gone better. I try to do the best I can. I am all by myself with my baby. You are still young, son, and have a long ways to go. Always remember when you're sick nobody ain't going to give you nothing. So try to stay healthy. Even without money your health is the best thing. I want you to promise me you will take a physic at least once a week as long as you live. Will you promise?"

"Yes, mother," I said.

"Good! Then hand me those pills in the top dresser drawer. They are in the box that says Coal Roller Pills. They're little bitty black pills."

The pills looked like Carter's Little Liver Pills, only they were about three times as black. After I had swallowed the three my mother handed me, the woman who had brought me said she had to leave.

"Now that your kid is here I've got to go home and cook my old man's supper."

When she had gone I asked mama if there was anything I could do for her.

"Yes," she said. "Look under the carpet and get that fifty cents. Go down to Zattermann's, on Rampart

Street, and get me a slice of meat, a pound of red beans and a pound of rice. Stop at Stahle's Bakery and buy two loaves of bread for a nickel. And hurry back, son."

It was the first time I had been out in the city without my grandma's guidance, and I was proud that my mother trusted me to go as far as Rampart Street. I was determined to do exactly as she said.

When I came out of the back court to the front of the house I saw a half a dozen ragged, snot-nosed kids standing on the sidewalk. I said hello to them very pleasantly.

After all I had come from James Alley which was a very tough spot and I had seen some pretty rough fellows. However, the boys in the Alley had been taught how to behave in a nice way and to respect other people. Everyone said good morning and good evening, asked their blessings before meals and said their prayers. Naturally I figured all the kids everywhere had the same training.

When they saw how clean and nicely dressed I was they crowded around me.

"Hey, you. Are you a mama's boy?" one of them asked.

"A mama's boy? What does that mean?" I asked.

"Yeah, that's what you are. A mama's boy."

"I don't understand. What do you mean?"

A big bully called One Eye Bud came pretty close up on me and looked over my white Lord Fauntleroy suit with its Buster Brown collar.

"So you don't understand, huh? Well, that's just too bad."

Then he scooped up a big handful of mud and threw it on the white suit I loved so much. I only had two. The other little ashy-legged, dirty-faced boys laughed while I stood there splattered with mud and rather puzzled what to do about it. I was young, but I saw the odds were against me; if I started a fight I knew I would be licked.

"What's the matter, mama's boy, don't you like it?" One Eye Bud asked me.

"No, I don't like it."

Then before I knew what I was doing, and before any of them could get ready, I jumped at him and smashed the little snot square in the mouth. I was scared and I hit as hard as I possibly could. I had his mouth and nose bleeding plenty. Those kids were so surprised by what I had done that they tore out as fast as they could go with One Eye Bud in the lead. I was too dumbfounded to run after them — and besides I didn't want to.

I was afraid Mayann would hear the commotion and hurt herself struggling out of bed. Luckily she did not, and I went off to do my errands.

When I came back mother's room was filled with visitors: a crowd of cousins I had never seen. Isaac Miles, Aaron Miles, Jerry Miles, Willie Miles, Louisa Miles, Sarah Ann Miles, Flora Miles (who was a baby) and Uncle Ike Miles were all waiting to see their new cousin, as they put it.

"Louis," my mother said, "I want you to meet some more of your family."

Gee, I thought, all of these people are my cousins?

Uncle Ike Miles was the father of all those kids. His wife had died and left them on his hands to support, and he did a good job. To take care of them he worked on the levees unloading boats. He did not make much money and his work was not regular, but most of the time he managed to keep the kids eating and put clean shirts on their backs. He lived in one room with all those children, and somehow or other he managed to pack them all in. He put as many in the bed as it would hold, and the rest slept on the floor. God bless Uncle Ike. If it weren't for him I do not know what Mama Lucy and I would have done because when Mayann got the urge to go out on the town we might not see her for days and days. When this happened she always dumped us into Uncle Ike's lap.

In his room I would sleep between Aaron and Isaac while Mama Lucy slept between Flora and Louisa. Because the kids were so lazy they would not wash their dishes we ate out of some tin pans Uncle Ike bought. They used to break china plates so they would not have to clean them.

Uncle Ike certainly had his hands full with those kids. They were about as worthless as any kids I have ever seen, but we grew up together just the same.

As I have said my mother always kept me and Mama Lucy physic minded.

"A slight physic once or twice a week," she used to say, "will throw off many symptoms and germs that congregate from nowheres in your stomach. We can't afford no doctor for fifty cents or a dollar."

With that money she could cook pots of red beans and rice, and with that regime we did not have any sickness at all. Of course a child who grew up in my part of New Orleans went barefooted practically all the time. We were bound to pick up a nail, a splinter or a piece of glass sometimes. But we were young, healthy and tough as old hell so a little thing like lockjaw did not stay with us a long time.

Mother and some of her neighbors would go to the railroad tracks and fill baskets with pepper grass. She would boil this until it got really gummy and rub it on the wound. Then within two or three hours we kids would get out of bed and be playing around the streets as though nothing had happened.

As the old saying goes, "the Lord takes care of fools," and just think of the dangers we kids were in at all times. In our neighborhood there were always a number of houses being torn down or built and they were full of such rubbish as tin cans, nails, boards, broken bottles and window panes. We used to play in these houses, and one of the games we played was War, because we had seen so much of it in the movies. Of course we did not know anything about it, but we decided to appoint officers of different ranks anyway. One Eye Bud made himself General of the Army. Then he made me Sergeant-at-Arms. When I asked him what I had to do he told me that whenever a man was wounded I had to go out on the battlefield and lead him off.

One day when I was taking a wounded comrade off the field a piece of slate fell off a roof and landed on my head. It knocked me out cold and shocked me so bad I got lockjaw. When I was taken home Mama Lucy and Mayann worked frantically boiling up herbs and roots which they applied to my head. Then they gave me a glass of Pluto Water, put me to bed and sweated me out good all night long. The next morning I was on my way to school just as though nothing had happened.

chapter 2

AFTER A WEEK OR TWO mother recovered and went to work for some rich white folks on Canal Street, back by the City Park cemeteries. I was happy to see her well again, and I began to notice what was going on around me, especially in the honky-tonks in the neighborhood because they were so different from those in James Alley, which only had a piano. On Liberty, Perdido, Franklin and Poydras there were honky-tonks at every corner and in each one of them musical instruments of all kinds were played. At the corner of the street where I lived was the famous Funky Butt Hall, where I first heard Buddy Bolden play. He was blowing up a storm.

That neighborhood certainly had a lot to offer. Of course, we kids were not allowed to go into the Funky Butt, but we could hear the orchestra from the sidewalk. In those days it was the routine when there was a ball for the band to play for at least a half hour in the front of the honky-tonk before going back into the hall to play for the dancers. This was done in all parts of the city to draw people into the hall, and it usually worked.

Old Buddy Bolden blew so hard that I used to wonder if I would ever have enough lung power to fill one of those cornets. All in all Buddy Bolden was a great musician, but I think he blew too hard. I will even go so far as to say that he did not blow correctly. In any case he finally went crazy. You can figure that out for yourself.

You really heard music when Bunk Johnson played the cornet with the Eagle Band. I was young, but I could tell the difference. These were the men in his orchestra:

> Bunk Johnson — cornet.
> Frankie Ducson — trombone.
> Bob Lyons — bass fiddle.
> Henry Zeno — drums.
> Bill Humphrey — clarinet.
> Danny Lewis — bass violin.

You heard real music when you heard these guys.

Of course Buddy Bolden had the biggest reputation, but even as a small kid I believed in finesse, even in music.

The king of all the musicians was Joe Oliver, the finest trumpeter who ever played in New Orleans. He had only one competitor. That was Bunk and he rivaled Oliver in tone only. No one had the fire and the endurance Joe had. No one in jazz has created as much music as he has. Almost everything important in music today came from him. That is why they called him "King," and he deserved the title. Musicians from all over the world used to come to hear Joe Oliver when he was playing at the Lincoln Gardens in Chicago, and he never failed to thrill them.

I was just a little punk kid when I first saw him, but his first words to me were nicer than everything that I've heard from any of the bigwigs of music.

Of course at the age of five I was not playing the trumpet, but there was something about the instrument that caught my ears. When I was in church and when I was "second lining" — that is, following the brass bands in parades — I started to listen carefully to the different instruments, noticing the things they played and how they played them. That is how I learned to distinguish the differences between Buddy Bolden, King Oliver and Bunk Johnson. Of the three Bunk Johnson had the most beautiful tone, the best imagination and the softest sense of phrasing.

Today people think that Bunk taught me to play

the trumpet because our tones are somewhat similar. That, however, is all that we have in common. To me Joe Oliver's tone is just as good as Bunk's. And he had such range and such wonderful creations in his soul! He created some of the most famous phrases you hear today, and trends to work from. As I said before, Bolden was a little too rough, and he did not move me at all.

Next to Oliver and Bunk were Buddy Petit, a Creole youngster, and Joe Johnson. Both played the cornet, and unluckily both died young. The world should have heard them.

Mayann enrolled me at the Fisk School, at the corner of Franklin and Perdido Streets. I was an active youngster and anxious to do the right thing, and I did not stay in the kindergarten long but was soon in the second grade. I could read the newspaper to the older folk in my neighborhood who helped mama to raise me. As I grew older I began to sell newspapers so as to help mother to make both ends meet. By running with the older boys I soon began to get hep to the tip. When we were not selling papers we shot dice for pennies or played a little coon can or blackjack. I got to be a pretty slick player and I could hold my own with the other kids. Some nights I would come home with my pockets loaded with pennies, nickels, dimes and even quarters. Mother, sister and I would have enough money to go shopping. Now and then I even bought mother a new dress, and occasionally I got myself a pair of short pants in one of the shops on Rampart Street. Of course I could not get a pair of shoes, but as we went barefoot that did not matter. Instead of a shirt I wore a blue cotton jumper, a kind of sport jacket worn over suspenders.

Before I lucked up on store trousers I used to wear my "stepfathers' " trousers, rolling them up from the bottom so that they looked like plus fours or knickers.

Mayann had enough "stepfathers" to furnish me with plenty of trousers. All I had to do was turn my back and a new "pappy" would appear. Some of them were fine guys, but others were low lives, particularly one named Albert. Slim was not much better, but the worst of all was Albert. One day Albert and my mother were sitting on the bank of the old basin canal near Galves Street quarreling about something while I was playing near by. Suddenly he called her a "black bitch" and knocked her into the water with a blow in her face. Then he walked off without even looking back. My God, was I frantic! While Mayann was screaming in the water, with her face all bloody, I began to holler for help at the top of my voice. People ran up and pulled her out, but what a moment that was! I have never forgiven that man, and if I ever see him again I will kill him. However, I have been in New Orleans many times since that day, and I have never run into him. Old timers tell me he is dead.

The nicest of my stepfathers — I can remember at least six — was Gabe. He was not as highly educated or as smart as the others, but he had good common sense. That was what counted for me in those days. I liked stepfather Gabe a lot. As for stepfather Slim, he was not a bad guy, but he drank too much. One day he would be nice, and the next he would beat Mayann up. Never when I was there, however. I never forgot the experience with stepfather Albert, and I would never let anyone lay a hand on my mother without doing my best to help her.

When Mayann took up with Slim I was getting to be a big boy. Everyday there were fights, fights between whores, toughs, and even children. Some house in the district was always being torn down, and plenty of bricks were handy. Whenever two guys got into a quarrel they would run to the nearest rubbish pile and start throwing bricks at each other. Seeing these fights going on all the time, we kids adopted the same method.

One morning at ten o'clock Slim and Mayann had started to fight at Gravier and Franklin Streets. While they were fighting they went down Franklin until they reached Kid Brown's honky-tonk. The porter was sweeping the place out and the door was open. Slim and Mayann stumbled, still fighting, into the bar, around the piano and on the dance floor in the rear. While this was going on a friend of mine named Cocaine Buddy rushed up to me as I was leaving school during recess.

"Hurry up, Dipper (that was my nickname — short for Dippermouth, from the piece called *Dipper-*

mouth Blues)," he said, "some guy is beating your mother up."

I dropped my books and tore off to the battle. When I got to Kid Brown's they were still at it fighting their way out into the street again.

"Leave my mother alone. Leave my mother alone," I shouted.

Since he did not stop an idea popped into my mind: get some bricks. It did not take me a minute, and when I started throwing the bricks at him I did not waste a one. As a pitcher Satchel Paige had nothing on me.

"Run like hell! Slim will jump you," everybody cried.

There was no danger. One of the bricks caught Slim in the side and he doubled up. He was not going to run after me or anyone else. His pain got worse and he had to be taken to the Charity Hospital near by. I have never seen Slim again. He was a pretty good blues player, but aside from that we did not have much in common. And I did not particularly like his style.

As I grew up around Liberty and Perdido I observed everything and everybody. I loved all those people and they loved me. The good ones and the bad ones all thought that Little Louis (as they called me) was O.K. I stayed in my place, I respected everybody and I was never rude or sassy. Mayann and grandmother taught me that. Of course my father did not have time to teach me anything; he was too busy chasing chippies.

My real dad was a sharp man, tall and handsome and well built. He made the chicks swoon when he marched by as the grand marshal in the Odd Fellows parade. I was very proud to see him in his uniform and his high hat with the beautiful streamer hanging down by his side. Yes, he was a fine figure of a man, my dad. Or at least that is the way he seemed to me as a kid when he strutted by like a peacock at the head of the Odd Fellows parade.

When Mayann was living with stepfather Tom he was working at the DeSoto Hotel on Barrone and Perdido Streets. When he came home he brought with him a lot of "broken arms" which were the left overs from the tables he served. From them Mayann would fix a delicious lunch for me which I took to school when her work kept her away from home all day long. When I undid these wonders in the schoolyard, all the kids would gather around me like hungry wolves. It did not take them long to discover what I had: the best steaks, chops, chicken, eggs, a little of everything that was good.

One day while I was eating my lunch the crowd of kids gathered around me suddenly backed away and scattered in all directions. Wondering what was going on, I raised my eyes and saw One Eye Bud and his gang, the same gang I had the fight with on the day mama sent me to the grocery on Rampart Street. I did not show any signs of being afraid and waited for them to come up close to me. I expected there would be trouble, but instead one of them spoke to me politely.

"Hello, Dipper."

"Hello, boys. How are you?" I answered as though I was not nervous. "Have a piece of my sandwich?"

They turned into my lunch as though they had not eaten for ages. That did not worry me. Bad as they were I was glad to see them enjoy themselves. Afterwards we became good friends and they never bothered me again. Not only that, but they saw to it that no one else bothered me either. They were tough kids, all right. And to think that they thought I was tough still tickles me pink right to this day.

Old Mrs. Martin was the caretaker of the Fisk School, and along with her husband she did a good job. They were loved by everybody in the neighborhood. Their family was a large one, and two of the boys turned out to be good and real popular musicians. Henry Martin was the drummer in the famous Kid Ory's band which Mrs. Cole engaged for her lawn parties. She ran them two or three times a week, and it was almost impossible to get in if Kid Ory's orchestra was playing. Kootchy Martin was a fine pianist, and the father played the violin beautifully. I do not remember the father very well because he left New Orleans when I was very young. He was involved in the terrible race riot in East Saint Louis and has never been heard from since.

My Life in New Orleans

My friend was Walter Martin. I got to know him very well because we used to work together in the good old honky-tonk days. Walter was a fine guy, and he had one of the nicest dispositions that's ever been in any human being.

Mrs. Martin had three beautiful daughters with light skins of the Creole type: Orleania, Alice and Wilhelmina. The two oldest married. I was in love with Wilhelmina, but the poor child died before I got up the nerve to tell her. She was so kind and sweet that she had loads of admirers. I had an inferiority complex and felt that I was not good enough for her. I would give anything to be able to see her again. When she smiled at me the whole world would light up. Old Mrs. Martin is still living, as spry as ever at eighty, God bless her. She always had some kind of consolation for the underdog who would rap at her door and she could always find a bite to eat for him somewhere.

Across the street from where we lived was Elder Cozy's church. He was the most popular preacher in the neighborhood and he attracted people from other parts of the city as well. I can still remember the night mama took me to his church. Elder Cozy started to get warmed up and then he hit his stride. It was not long before he had the whole church rocking. Mama got so happy and so excited that she knocked me off the bench as she shouted and swayed back and forth. She was a stout woman and she became so excited that it took six of the strongest brothers to grab hold of her and

[31]

pacify her. I was just a kid and I did not dig at that time. I laughed myself silly, and when mama and I reached home she gave me hell.

"You little fool," she said. "What did you mean by laughing when you saw me being converted?"

After that mama really got religion. I saw her baptized in the Mississippi where she was ducked in the water so many times that I thought she was going to be drowned. The baptism worked: Mayann kept her religion.

When I sold papers I got them from a fine white boy named Charles, who was about four years older than I. He thought a lot of me, and he used to give me advice about life and how to take care of myself. I told him about the little quartet in which I sang and about how much money we made when we passed the hat. He was worried because I was going down to the red-light district at my age and singing for pimps and whores. I explained that there was more money to be made there, and that the people were crazy about our singing. This reassured him. I continued to sell papers for Charles until I was arrested on a New Year's Day for carrying an old pistol which one of my stepfathers had hidden in the house during the celebration.

chapter 3

NEW ORLEANS CELEBRATES the period from Christmas through the New Year jubilantly, with torch light processions and firing off Roman candles. In those days we used to shoot off guns and pistols or anything loud so as to make as much noise as possible. Guns, of course, were not allowed officially, and we had to keep an eye on the police to see that we were not pulled in for toting one. That is precisely what happened to me, and as a matter of fact that is what taught me how to play the trumpet.

I had found that .38 pistol in the bottom of Mayann's old cedar trunk. Naturally she did not know that

I had taken it with me that night when I went out to sing.

First I must explain how our quartet used to do its hustling so as to attract an audience. We began by walking down Rampart Street between Perdido and Gravier. The lead singer and the tenor walked together in front followed by the baritone and the bass. Singing at random we wandered through the streets until someone called to us to sing a few songs. Afterwards we would pass our hats and at the end of the night we would divvy up. Most of the time we would draw down a nice little taste. Then I would make a bee line for home and dump my share into mama's lap.

Little Mack, our lead singer, later became one of the best drummers in New Orleans. Big Nose Sidney was the bass. Redhead Happy Bolton was the baritone. Happy was also a drummer and the greatest showman of them all, as all the old-timers will tell you. As for me, I was the tenor. I used to put my hand behind my ear, and move my mouth from side to side, and some beautiful tones would appear. Being young, I had a high voice and it stayed that way until I got out of the orphanage into which I was about to be thrown.

As usual we were walking down Rampart Street, just singing and minding our own business, when all of a sudden a guy on the opposite side of the street pulled out a little old six-shooter pistol and fired it off. *Dy-Dy-Dy-Dy-Dy-Dy.*

"Go get him, Dipper," my gang said.

[34]

Without hesitating I pulled out my stepfather's revolver from my bosom and raised my arm into the air and let her go. Mine was a better gun than the kid's and the six shots made more noise. The kid was frightened and cut out and was out of sight like a jack rabbit. We all laughed about it and started down the street again, singing as we walked along.

Further down on Rampart Street I reloaded my gun and started to shoot again up into the air, to the great thrill of my companions. I had just finished firing my last blank cartridge when a couple of strong arms came from behind me. It was cold enough that night, but I broke out into a sweat that was even colder. My companions cut out and left me, and I turned around to see a tall white detective who had been watching me fire my gun. Oh boy! I started crying and making all kinds of excuses.

"Please, mister, don't arrest me. . . I won't do it no more. . . Please. . . Let me go back to mama. . . I won't do it no more."

It was no use. The man did not let me go. I was taken to the Juvenile Court, and then locked up in a cell where, sick and disheartened, I slept on a hard bed until the next morning.

I was frightened when I woke. What were they going to do to me? Where were they going to send me? I had no idea what a Waifs' Home was. How long would I have to stay there? How serious was it to fire off a pistol in the street? Oh, I had a million minds,

[35]

and I could not pacify any of them. I was scared, more scared than I was the day Jack Johnson knocked out Jim Jeffries. That day I was going to get my supply of papers from Charlie, who employed a good many colored boys like myself. On Canal Street I saw a crowd of colored boys running like mad toward me.

I asked one of them what had happened.

"You better get started, black boy," he said breathlessly as he started to pull me along. "Jack Johnson has just knocked out Jim Jeffries. The white boys are sore about it and they're going to take it out on us."

He did not have to do any urging. I lit out and passed the other boys in a flash. I was a fast runner, and when the other boys reached our neighborhood I was at home looking calmly out of the window. The next day the excitement had blown over.

But to return to the cell in which they had kept me all night for celebrating with my stepfather's old .38 revolver, the door was opened about ten o'clock by a man carrying a bunch of keys.

"Louis Armstrong?" he asked.

"Yes, sir."

"This way. You are going out to the Colored Waifs' Home for Boys."

When I went out in the yard a wagon like the Black Maria at the House of Detention was waiting with two fine horses to pull it. A door with a little bitty grilled window was slammed behind me and away I went, along with several other youngsters who had been arrested for doing the same thing I had done.

The Waifs' Home was an old building which had apparently formerly been used for another purpose. It was located in the country opposite a great big dairy farm where hundreds of cows, bulls, calves and a few horses were standing. Some were eating, and some prancing around like they wanted to tell somebody, anybody, how good they felt. The average square would automatically say those animals were all loco, to be running like that, but for me they wanted to express themselves as being very happy, gay, and contented.

When I got out of the wagon with the other boys the first thing I noticed was several large trees standing before the building. A very lovely odor was swinging across my nostrils.

"What flowers are those that smell so good?" I asked.

"Honeysuckles," was the answer.

I fell in love with them, and I'm ready to get a whiff of them any time.

The inmates were having their lunch. We walked down a long corridor leading to the mess hall where a long line of boys was seated eating white beans without rice out of tin plates. They gave me the rooky greeting saying, "Welcome, newcomer. Welcome to your new home." I was too depressed to answer. When I sat down at the end of the table I saw a plate full of

beans being passed in my direction. In times that I
didn't have a care in the world I would have annihilated
those beans. But this time I only pushed them away.
I did the same thing for several days. The keepers, Mr.
and Mrs. Jones and Mr. Alexander and Mr. Peter
Davis, saw me refuse these meals, but they did not say
anything about it. On the fourth day I was so hungry
I was first at the table. Mr. Jones and his colleagues
gave me a big laugh. I replied with a sheepish grin.
I did not share their sense of humor; it did not blend
with mine.

The keepers were all colored. Mr. Jones, a young
man who had recently served in the cavalry, drilled us
every morning in the court in front of the Waifs'
Home, and we were taught the manual of arms with
wooden guns.

Mr. Alexander taught the boys how to do carpen-
try, how to garden and how to build camp fires. Mr.
Peter Davis taught music and gave vocational training.
Each boy had the right to choose the vocation which
interested him.

Quite naturally I would make a bee line to Mr.
Davis and his music. Music has been in my blood from
the day I was born. Unluckily at first I did not get on
very well with Mr. Davis because he did not like the
neighborhood I came from. He thought that only the
toughest kids came from Liberty and Perdido Streets.
They were full of honky-tonks, toughs and fancy women. Furthermore, the Fisk School had a bad reputa-

tion. Mr. Davis thought that since I had been raised in such bad company I must also be worthless. From the start he gave me a very hard way to go, and I kept my distance. One day I broke an unimportant rule, and he gave me fifteen hard lashes on the hand. After that I was really scared of him for a long time.

Our life was regulated by bugle calls. A kid blew a bugle for us to get up, to go to bed and to come to meals. The last call was the favorite with us all. Whether they were cutting trees a mile away or building a fire under the great kettle in the yard to scald our dirty clothes, the boys would hot foot it back to the Home when they heard the mess call. I envied the bugler because he had more chances to use his instrument than anyone else.

When the orchestra practiced with Mr. Davis, who was a good teacher, I listened very carefully, but I did not dare go near the band though I wanted to in the worst way. I was afraid Mr. Davis would bawl me out or give me a few more lashes. He made me feel he hated the ground I walked on, so I would sit in a corner and listen, enjoying myself immensely.

The little brass band was very good, and Mr. Davis made the boys play a little of every kind of music. I had never tried to play the cornet, but while listening to the band every day I remembered Joe Oliver, Bolden and Bunk Johnson. And I had an awful urge to learn the cornet. But Mr. Davis hated me. Furthermore I did not know how long they were going to keep me at

the Home. The judge had condemned me for an in-
definite period which meant that I would have to stay
there until he set me free or until some important white
person vouched for me and for my mother and father.
That was my only chance of getting out of the Waifs'
Home fast. So I had plenty of time to listen to the band
and wish I could learn to play the cornet.

Finally, through Mr. Jones, I got a chance to sing
in the school. My first teacher was Miss Spriggins.
Then I was sent to Mrs. Vigne, who taught the higher
grades.

As the days rolled by, Mr. Davis commenced to
lighten up on his hatred of me. Occasionally I would
catch his eye meeting with mine. I would turn away,
but he would catch them again and give me a slight
smile of approval which would make me feel good inside. From then on whenever Mr. Davis spoke to me
or smiled I was happy. Gee, what a feeling — that coming from him! I was beginning to adapt myself to the
place, and since I had to stay there for a long time I
thought I might as well adjust myself. I did.

Six months went by. We were having supper of
black molasses and a big hunk of bread which after all
that time seemed just as good as a home cooked chicken
dinner. Just as we were about to get up from the table
Mr. Davis slowly came over and stopped by me.

"Louis Armstrong," he said, "how would you like
to join our brass band?"

I was so speechless and so surprised I just could

not answer him right away. To make sure that I had understood him he repeated his question.

"Louis Armstrong, I asked if you would like to join *our* brass band."

"I certainly would, Mr. Davis. I certainly would," I stammered.

He patted me on the back and said:

"Wash up and come to rehearsal."

While I was washing I could not think of anything but of my good luck in finally getting a chance to play the cornet. I got soap in my eyes but didn't pay any attention to it. I thought of what the gang would say when they saw me pass through the neighborhood blowing a cornet. I already pictured myself playing with all the power and endurance of a Bunk, Joe or Bolden. When I was washed I rushed to the rehearsal.

"Here I am, Mr. Davis."

To my surprise he handed me a tambourine, the little thing you tap with your fingers like a miniature drum. So that was the end of my beautiful dream! But I did not say a word. Taking the tambourine, I started to whip it in rhythm with the band. Mr. Davis was so impressed he immediately changed me to the drums. He must have sensed that I had the beat he was looking for.

They were playing *At the Animals' Ball*, a tune that was very popular in those days and which had a break right in the channel. When the break came I made it a real good one and a fly one at that. All the boys yelled "Hooray for Louis Armstrong." Mr. Davis nodded with approval which was all I needed. His approval was all important for any boy who wanted a musical career.

"You are very good, Louis," he said. "But I need an alto player. How about trying your luck?"

"Anything you like, Mr. Davis," I answered with all the confidence in the world.

He handed me an alto. I had been singing for a number of years and my instinct told me that an alto takes a part in a band same as a baritone or tenor in a quartet. I played my part on the alto very well.

As soon as the rehearsal was over, the bugle blew for bed. All the boys fell into line and were drilled up to the dormitory by the band. In the dormitory we could talk until nine o'clock when the lights were turned out and everybody had to be quiet and go to sleep. Nevertheless we used to whisper in low voices taking care we did not attract the attention of the keepers who slept downstairs near Mr. and Mrs. Jones. Somebody would catch a licking if we talked too loud and brought one of the keepers upstairs.

In the morning when the bugle blew *I Can't Get 'Em Up* we jumped out of bed and dressed as quickly as possible because our time was limited. They knew just how long it should take, they'd been in the business so long. If any one was late he had to have a good excuse or he would have to hold out his hand for a lashing.

It was useless to try to run away from the Waifs'

Home. Anyone who did was caught in less than a week's time. One night while we were asleep a boy tied about half a dozen sheets together. He greased his body so that he could slip through the wooden bars around the dormitory. He let himself down to the ground and disappeared. None of us understood how he had succeeded in doing it, and we were scared to death that we would be whipped for having helped him. On the contrary, nothing happened. All the keepers said after his disappearance was:

"He'll be back soon."

They were right. He was caught and brought back in less than a week. He was all nasty and dirty from sleeping under old houses and wherever else he could and eating what little he could scrounge. The police had caught him and turned him over to the Juvenile Court.

Not a word was said to him during the first day he was back. We all wondered what they were going to do to him, and we thought that perhaps they were going to give him a break. When the day was over the bugle boy sounded taps, and we all went up to the dormitory. The keepers waited until we were all undressed and ready to put on our pajamas.

At that moment Mr. Jones shouted:

"Hold it, boys."

Then he looked at the kid who had run away.

"I want everyone to put on their pajamas except

that young man. He ran away, and he has to pay for it."

We all cried, but it was useless. Mr. Jones called the four strongest boys in the dormitory to help him. He made two of them hold the culprit's legs and the other two his arms in such a way that he could only move his buttocks. To these writhing naked buttocks Mr. Jones gave one hundred and five lashes. All of the boys hollered, but the more we hollered the harder he hit. It was a terrible thing to watch the poor kid suffer. He could not sit down for over two weeks.

I saw several fools try to run away, but after what happened to that first boy I declined the idea.

One day we were out on the railroad tracks picking up worn-out ties which the railroad company gave to the Waifs' Home for fire wood. Two boys were needed to carry each tie. In our bunch was a boy of about eighteen from a little Louisiana town called Houma. You could tell he was a real country boy by the way he murdered the King's English. We called him Houma after his home town.

We were on our way back to the Home, which was about a mile down the road. Among us was a boy about eighteen or nineteen years old named Willie Davis and he was the fastest runner in the place. Any kid who thought he could outrun Willie Davis was crazy. But the country boy did not know what a good runner Davis was.

About a half mile from the Home we heard one

of the ties drop. Before we realized what had happened we saw Houma sprinting down the road, but he was headed in the wrong direction. When he was about a hundred yards away Mr. Alexander saw him and called Willie Davis.

"Go get him, Willie."

Willie was after Houma like a streak of lightning while we all stood open-mouthed, wondering if Willie would be able to catch up. Houma speeded up a little when he saw that Willie was after him, but he was no match for the champ and Willie soon caught him.

Here is the pay-off.

When Willie slapped his hand on Houma's shoulder and stopped him, Willie said:

"Come on kid. You gotta go back."

"What's the matter?" Houma said. "Ah wasn't gwine no whars."

After the five hundred lashes Houma did not try to run away again. Finally some important white folks for whom Houma's parents worked sent for the kid and had him shipped back home with an honorable discharge. We got a good laugh out of that one. "Ah wasn't gwine no whars."

As time went on I commenced being the most popular boy in the Home. Seeing how much Mr. Davis liked me and the amount of time he gave me, the boys began to warm up to me and take me into their confidence.

One day the young bugler's mother and father,

who had gotten his release, came to take him home. The minute he left Mr. Davis gave me his place. I took up the bugle at once and began to shine it up. The other bugler had never shined the instrument and the brass was dirty and green. The kids gave me a big hand when they saw the gleaming bright instrument instead of the old filthy green one.

I felt real proud of my position as bugler. I would stand very erect as I would put the bugle nonchalantly to my lips and blow real mellow tones. The whole place seemed to change. Satisfied with my tone Mr. Davis gave me a cornet and taught me how to play *Home, Sweet Home.* Then I was in seventh heaven. Unless I was dreaming, my ambition had been realized.

Every day I practiced faithfully on the lesson Mr. Davis gave me. I became so good on the cornet that one day Mr. Davis said to me:

"Louis, I am going to make you leader of the band."

I jumped straight into the air, with Mr. Davis watching me, and ran to the mess room to tell the boys the good news. They were all rejoiced with me. Now at last I was not only a musician but a band leader! Now I would get a chance to go out in the streets and see Mayann and the gang that hung around Liberty and Perdido Streets. The band often got a chance to play at a private picnic or join one of the frequent parades through the streets of New Orleans covering all parts of the city, Uptown, Back o' Town, Front o' Town, Downtown. The band was even sent to play in the West End and Spanish Fort, our popular summer resorts, and also at Milenburg and Little Woods.

The band's uniform consisted of long white pants turned up to look like knickers, black easy-walkers, or sneakers as they are now called, thin blue gabardine coats, black stockings and caps with black and white bands which looked very good on the young musicians. To stand out as the leader of the band I wore cream colored pants, brown stockings, brown easy-walkers and a cream colored cap.

In those days some of the social clubs paraded all day long. When the big bands consisting of old-timers complained about such a tiresome job, the club members called on us.

"Those boys," they said, "will march all day long and won't squawk one bit."

They were right. We were so glad to get a chance to walk in the street that we did not care how long we paraded or how far. The day we were engaged by the Merry-Go-Round Social Club we walked all the way to Carrolton, a distance of about twenty-five miles. Playing like mad, we loved every foot of the trip.

The first day we paraded through my old neighborhood everybody was gathered on the sidewalks to see us pass. All the whores, pimps, gamblers, thieves and beggars were waiting for the band because they knew that Dipper, Mayann's son, would be in it. But they had never dreamed that I would be playing the cornet, blowing it as good as I did. They ran to wake up mama, who was sleeping after a night job, so she could see me go by. Then they asked Mr. Davis if they could give me some money. He nodded his head with approval, not thinking that the money would amount to very much. But he did not know that sporting crowd. Those sports gave me so much that I had to borrow the hats of several other boys to hold it all. I took in enough to buy new uniforms and new instruments for everybody who played in the band. The instruments we had been using were old and badly battered.

This increased my popularity at the Home, and Mr. Davis gave me permission to go into town by myself to visit Mayann. He and Mr. and Mrs. Jones probably felt that this was the best way to show their gratitude.

One day we went to play at a white folks' picnic at Spanish Fort near West End. There were picnics there every Sunday for which string orchestras were hired or occasionally a brass band. When all the bands were busy we used to be called on.

On that day we decided to take a swim during the intermission since the cottage at which we were playing was on the edge of the water. We were swimming and having a lot of fun when Jimmy's bathing trunks fell off. While we were hurrying to fish them out of the water a white man took a shot gun off the rack on the porch. As Jimmy was struggling frantically to pull his trunks on again the white man aimed the shot gun at him and said:

"You black sonofabitch, cover up that black ass of yours or I'll shoot."

We were scared stiff, but the man and his party broke out laughing and it all turned out to be a huge joke. We were not much good the rest of that day, but we weren't so scared that we could not eat all the spaghetti and beer they gave us when they were through eating. It was good.

Among the funny incidents that happened at the Home I will never forget the stunt Red Sun pulled off. He had been sent to the Home for stealing. It was a mania with him; he would steal everything which was not nailed down. Before I ever saw the Home he had served two or three terms there. He would be released, and two or three months later he would be back again to serve another term for stealing.

After serving six months while I was at the Home he was paroled by the judge. Three months passed, and he was still out on the streets. We took it for granted that Red Sun had gone straight at last and we practically forgot all about him.

One day while Mr. Jones was drilling us in front of the Home we saw somebody coming down the road riding on a real beautiful horse. We all wondered who it could be. Mr. Jones stopped the drill and waited with us while we watched the horse and rider come towards us. To our amazement it was Red Sun. Above all he was riding bareback. We crowded around to tell how glad we were to see him looking so good and to admire his horse.

"Where did you get that fine looking horse, Red?" Mr. Jones asked.

Red, who was very ugly, gave a very pleasant smile.

"I have been working," he said. "I had such a good job that I was able to buy the horse. What do you think of him?"

Mr. Jones thought he was pretty and so did all the rest of us. Red poked his chest way out.

He spent the whole day with us, letting us all take turns riding his horse. Oh, we had a ball! Red stayed for supper, the same as I did in later years, and when I blew the bugle for taps he mounted his fine horse and bade us all good-bye.

"Ah'll see you-all soon," he said and he rode away as good as the Lone Ranger. After he had left, Red was the topic of conversation until the lights went out. We all went to sleep saying how great ol' Red Sun had become.

After dinner the next evening while we were looking out the windows we saw Mr. Alexander — he generally went to the Juvenile Court for delinquents — bring a new recruit into Mr. Jones' office. We wondered who it could be: it was Red Sun — bless my lamb — who had been arrested for stealing a horse.

I saw plenty of miserable kids brought into the Home. One day a couple of small kids had been picked up in the streets of New Orleans covered with body lice and head lice. Out in the back yard there was an immense kettle which was used to boil up our dirty clothes. Those two kids were in such a filthy condition that we had to shave their heads and throw their clothes into the fire underneath the kettle.

The Waifs' Home was surely a very clean place, and we did all the work ourselves. That's where I learned how to scrub floors, wash and iron, cook, make up beds, do a little of everything around the house. The first thing we did to a newcomer was to make him take a good shower, and his head and body were carefully examined to see that he did not bring any vermin into the Home. Every day we had to line up for inspection.

Anyone whose clothes were not in proper condition was pulled out of line and made to fix them himself. Once a week we were given a physic, when we lined up in the morning, and very few of the boys were sick. The place was more like a health center or a boarding school than a boys' jail. We played all kinds of sports, and we turned out some mighty fine baseball players, swimmers and musicians. All in all I am proud of the days I spent at the Colored Waifs' Home for Boys.

chapter 4

I WAS FOURTEEN when I left the Home. My father was still working in the turpentine factory and he had his boss have a talk with Judge Wilson. I was released on the condition that I would live with my father and stepmother. They came to get me on a beautiful evening in June when the air was heavy with the odor of honeysuckle. How I loved that smell! On quiet Sunday nights when I lay on my bunk listening to Freddie Keppard and his jazz band play for some rich white folks about half a mile away, the perfume of those delicious flowers roamed about my nostrils.

On the day my father and stepmother were coming

to take me to their home I thought about what lay ahead. The first thing that came into my mind was that I would no longer be able to listen to Freddie Keppard. He was a good cornet man with a beautiful tone and marvelous endurance. He had a style of his own. Of course Bunk Johnson had the best tone of all, but Freddie had his own little traits which always interested and amused me. Whenever he played in a street parade he used to cover his fingers with a pocket handkerchief so that the other cornet players wouldn't catch his stuff. Silly, I thought, but that was Freddie, and everybody ate it up. There was no doubt about it, he had talent.

Those nights when I lay on my bunk listening to Freddie play the cornet and smelling the honeysuckles were really heaven for a kid of my age. I hated to think I was going to have to leave it.

I wondered what my father would say if I asked him to let me stay in the Home. After all, I had never lived with him, and I did not even know his wife. What kind of a woman was she? Would we get on together? What kind of a disposition did she have? Here at the Home I'd become happy. Everybody there loved me, and I was in love with everybody. At my father's house would I still see Mayann and Mama Lucy who came to see me three times a week? My father had never paid me a single visit. What about the boys and even the keepers? They all looked sad, their faces drawn, to see me leave, and I felt the same way about them.

While my things were being packed the little band played as it had never played before. I played several numbers with them for my father's approval. He was elated by the progress his son had made, and he said I should keep it up.

Mrs. Jones kissed me good-bye, and I shook hands with every kid in the place as well as with Mr. Jones, Mr. Davis and Mr. Alexander. I was unhappy when we left the Home and walked to City Park Avenue to take the street car into town.

My father and stepmother lived at Miro and Poydras Streets, right in the heart of The Battlefield. They were happily married and they had two boys, Willie and Henry. I did not have to wonder long about Gertrude, my stepmother, because she turned out to be a very fine woman, and she treated me just as though I were her own child. For that alone I will always love her. Henry was nice too. He was very kind to me at all times and we became good friends. His older brother, however, was about as ornery as they come. He deliberately would do everything he could to upset everybody.

After living with them for a while, my parents, who both had jobs, discovered that I could cook and that I could make particularly good beans. They were therefore glad to leave me with the two boys and to let me cook for them. Since I was the oldest they thought the kids would obey me. Henry did. But oh, that Willie! He was such a terrible liar that sometimes I wanted to throw a whole pot of beans at his head. He knew that his parents would swallow half of the lies he told them. What is more, they did not whip him much.

One day he did something so bad that nothing in the world could have kept me from hitting him in the face. It was a hard blow and it hurt him. I was afraid that after he told Pa Willie and Ma Gertrude when they came home they would send me back to the Home. But the little brat did not even open his mouth to them. I guess he realized he was in the wrong and that he deserved his chastising.

They used to laugh like mad when I first began to practice my cornet. Then as the days went on they began to listen and to make little comments, the way kids will. Then we began to understand one another. They were growing rapidly, and the more they grew the more they ate. I soon learned what a capacity they had, and I learned to take precautions. Whenever I cooked a big pot of beans and rice and ham hocks they would manage to eat up most of it before I could get to the table. Willie could make a plate full of food vanish faster than anyone I ever saw.

I soon got wise to those two boys. Whenever I cooked I would see to it that I ate my bellyful before I rang the bell for Willie and Henry to come in from the yard. One day Willie asked me why I was not eating with them. I told him I had to taste my cooking while I cooked it and that after it was done I didn't have any appetite. They fell for it, hook, line and sinker.

While I was staying with Pa Willie and Ma Gertrude my little stepsister Gertrude was born. I left shortly afterwards because father decided that he was just earning enough to support his three children by my stepmother. In those days common laborers were badly paid, and though both Pa and Ma Gertrude were working they could barely make both ends meet.

My real mother came out there one evening, and she and Pa talked things over for a long time. When Mayann got ready to leave, my father said:

"Louis, would you like to go home with your mother?"

I was thrilled to hear this, but I didn't want him to know it. He had tried his best to make me happy while I was living with him, Gertrude and the two boys. I was ever so grateful for that and their kindness.

"O.K. Pa. I love both you and Mayann, and I will come to see you often."

"He's a fine kid," he said to Mayann, smiling and patting me on the shoulder.

"He sure is," she said. Then we went out the door for Liberty and Perdido Streets, my old stomping grounds.

The next morning I waked up bright and early and went out to look for my old gang, my schoolmates, or anyone I used to know.

The first person I ran into was Cocaine Buddy

Martin, whose sister Bella I used to sweetheart. He had
grown a good deal and was wearing long pants. He had
a job with Joe Segretta, who ran a combination grocery,
saloon and honky-tonk.

I slipped up behind him when he was sweeping
out the joint from the night's gappings and happenings,
and put my hands over his eyes.

"Guess who?"

He couldn't guess. When I took my hands away
he gave a big glad yell:

"Dipper! Man, you've been gone a long, long
time."

He did not know that I had been out of the Waifs'
Home for a long time and that I had been staying at
my father's house and cooking for my little step-
brothers.

"Well, that's good," Cocaine Buddy said. "It
didn't look like they was ever going to turn you loose
from the Waifs' Home."

We laughed it off and then I asked Buddy what's
what.

"Oh, I almost forgot. You play the cornet don't
you? Isn't that what they call the thing you blow?"

"Yes, I play the cornet, Buddy. But I don't know
if I am good enough to play in a regular band."

"I think you are good enough to hold down this
job I'm talking about."

I asked him where.

"Right over there," he said pointing across the

street to a honky-tonk. "The boss man's name is Henry Ponce. He is one of the biggest operators in the red-light district, and he ain't scared of nobody. He wants a good cornet player. If you think you can handle it I'll speak a good word for you. All you have to do is to put on your long pants and play the blues for the whores that hustle all night. They come in with a big stack of money in their stockings for their pimps. When you play the blues they will call you sweet names and buy you drinks and give you tips."

Thinking of Mayann and Mama Lucy who badly needed help I said: "Try your luck, Buddy. See if you can get that job for me."

It was a curious thing, but Buddy did not tell me Henry Ponce and Joe Segretta were deadly enemies. Segretta was Italian; Ponce, French; and both of them handled a lot of money and a lot of business. They were tough characters and one would try to outdo the other in every respect.

Buddy got the job for me, and after I had been working there for about six months the relationship between the two white men got exceedingly tense. I never knew exactly just what the cause of their quarrel was.

Saturday the tonk stayed open all night, and on Sunday I did not leave before ten or eleven in the morning. The drunks would spend a lot of money and the tips were good as tips went in those days. I saved money all around. Mayann would fix me a big bucket lunch to take to the tonk and eat in the early hours. This saved me the expense of eating at a lunch counter or lunch wagon. Mayann said that the meals in those places were not worth the money they cost, and I agreed with her.

I was young and strong and had all the ambition in the world and I wanted to do whole lots to help Mayann and Mama Lucy. After I got set at Henry Ponce's place, I got another job driving a coal cart during the day. After I had finished work at four in the morning I would run back home and grab a couple of hours' sleep. Then I would go to the C. A. Andrews Coal Company at Ferret and Perdido Streets two blocks away from the honky-tonk. From seven in the morning to five in the evening I would haul hard coal at fifteen cents per load. And I loved it. I was fifteen years old, and I felt like a real man when I shoveled a ton of coal into my wagon. Being as young and small as I was I could not make over five loads a day. But I was not doing so bad. The seventy-five cents I made in the day plus the dollar and a quarter plus tips I made in the tonk added up. Then the owners of other honky-tonks commenced bidding for my services. Gee, I really thought I was somebody then. However, I would not give up my mule and my coal wagon.

One reason I liked to drive the coal wagon was my stepdaddy, Mr. Gabe. He was an old hand at the Andrews Coal Company and he also got me my job there; he was the stepdaddy I liked best. He drove a wagon with two mules and he got paid thirty cents a load, three times as much as I got. He knew all the tricks of the trade and he could deliver nine, ten and sometimes more loads a day. He taught me the knack of loading up a cart so I would not hurt my back so much. In those days it was a good thing to have a steady job because there was always the chance that the cops might close the tonk down any minute. In case that happened I would still have money coming in.

As a matter of fact it was not long before the tonk where I worked was closed down. That was when I really found out what Joe Segretta and Henry Ponce were feuding about. It was Sunday morning and everybody had left except that good-looking Frenchman and me. Ponce had walked to the door with me talking about some blues our band had played that night. This surprised me because I had no idea he was paying any attention at all.

When I reached the sidewalk I turned around to continue beating my chops with Ponce, who was standing in the doorway. After about ten minutes I casually noticed several colored guys, who hung around Joe Segretta's, standing before Gasper's grocery store on the corner opposite Segretta's and Ponce's tonks — all of them tough guys and all of them working for Joe Segretta. They were out to get Ponce. But Ponce, who was pretty tough himself, wasn't aware of this. Nor was I. All of a sudden I saw one of them pull out his gun and point it at us. He shot twice and tore off toward Howard and Perdido Streets just a block away. Then before we could dig what was going on, these tough guys started shooting.

"Well, I'll be goddamned," Ponce said as they emptied their guns and started to run, "those black bastards are shooting at me."

Ponce whipped a revolver out of his bosom and started after them. When he reached Howard and Perdido Streets I heard six shots fired one right after the other. While the shots were being fired at Ponce I had not moved and the flock of bystanders who saw me riveted to the sidewalk rushed up to me.

"Were you hit?" they asked. "Are you hurt?"

When they asked me what they did, I fainted. It suddenly made me conscious of the danger I had been in. I thought the first shot had hit me.

When I came to I could still hear the shots coming from Howard and Perdido and the cries of the colored boys. They were no match for Ponce; he was shooting well and he wounded each of them. When he stopped shooting he walked back to his saloon raging mad and swearing to himself.

The three colored boys were taken off to the Charity Hospital for treatment, and I was carried back to Mayann. It was days before I got over the shock.

After that little scrimmage that gang never did bother Henry Ponce again; they were all convinced he was a real tough customer. I continued to work in his honky-tonk, but I was always on the alert, thinking something would jump off any minute. However nothing happened, and finally during one of the election campaigns all of the honky-tonks were closed down. Henry Ponce, like the rest of the honky-tonk owners, had every intention of opening up again when things blew over, but the law kept us closed so long that he got discouraged and went into business downtown.

chapter 5

I THINK THAT HENRY PONCE went into men's haberdashery or some other kind of legitimate business. At any rate he could not use me, and I never saw him again. We all missed Henry Ponce because he was a kind and generous man, and many a time I have seen him stop on the street to slip a little change to any old raggedy underdog. That was something to do in those days in the South.

Of course I still had my job on the coal wagon when Henry Ponce closed down. I could go home early and get some rest at night. Many nights, however, after eating supper and washing up I would put on the tailor-made long pants I had saved up for a long time. Then Isaac Smooth and I would make the round of the honky-tonks watching the people and laughing at the drunks. The bouncers left them alone if they fell asleep propped against the wall, but if they collapsed or started raising hell they were thrown out pronto. We would dig that jive and watch the whores, who would often get into quarrels over the same pimp and fight like mad dogs.

Isaac Smooth, or Ike as we called him, and I had been in the Waifs' Home together and we had both played in the band. He was a very handsome child, and a lot of the whores would try to make him. Like me he was afraid of those bad, strong women. Our mothers had warned us about them, and we did not think too much about sex. We wanted to learn all we could about life, but mostly we were interested in music. We were always looking for a new piano player with something new on the ball like a rhythm that was all his own. These fellows with real talent often came from the levee camps. They'd sit on a piano stool and beat out some of the damnedest blues you ever heard in your life. And when Ike and I discovered one we were the two happiest kids in New Orleans.

The most popular tonk was at the corner of Gravier and Franklin, and there I saw a fight between two whores that will never leave my memory. The fight was over a pimp, and the two whores were Mary Jack the Bear and a girl I'll call Deborah. Mary

Louis Armstrong, his mother Mayann *(seated)*, his sister
Mama Lucy.

(Courtesy E. H. Sanfiel

The site of Louis' grandmother's house, showing the Chinaball trees fro which Louis would cut the switches his grandmother used to punish hir

Joseph Jones, who taught Louis Armstrong to play a bugle holding the instrument on which Louis learned.

(Courtesy Rudi Blesh)

The Superior Brass Band, with Bunk Johnson *(second from left, standing).*

"King" Oliver, about 1915.

Freddy Keppard, about 1916.

urtesy Rudi Blesh)

(Courtesy Rudi Blesh)

Tom Anderson's in Story-
ville, New Orleans, at the
corner of Sherville and
Anderson Streets.

The start of a New Orleans funeral.

Louis Armstrong as King of the Zulus, 1949, with his niece
(left) and his grandmother *(right)*.

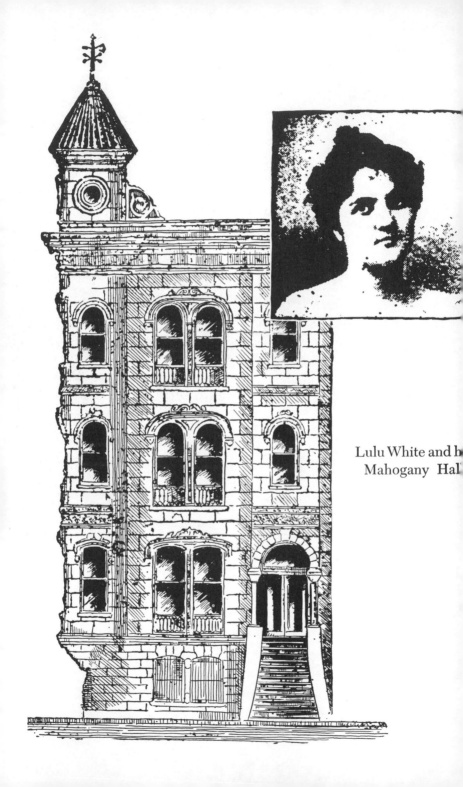

Lulu White and h[...]
Mahogany Hal[...]

On the river boat *Sydney*, 1918. *Left to right:* Baby Dodds, William Ridgely, Joe Howard, Louis Armstrong, Fate Marable, David Jones, Johnny Dodds, Johnny St. Cyr, Pops Foster.

King Oliver's Creole Jazz Band, Lincoln Gardens, Chicago. *Left to right:* Honore Dutrey, Baby Dodds, Joe Oliver, Lil Hardin, Bill Johnson, Johnny Dodds, Louis Armstrong *(kneeling in front).*

Jack was the toughest woman in all the tonks. Pretty Deborah was just a plain good-looking girl right out of high school. Where she came from, I don't know, but she sure was attractive. She fell in love with Mary Jack's pimp who put her on the street. Deborah did not mind this, for she was as deeply in love with the pimp as Mary Jack. Deborah had never heard about her rival, and she did not know that they were both sharing the same pimp. Mary Jack did not know either — not until that drizzling New Year's night when the celebrating was just about over.

They were both half tipsy when they met in the tonk where the pimp was drinking with Deborah. Mary Jack commenced signifying with some nasty remarks.

"Some old bitch in this bar is going with my man. She gives him all the money she makes and he brings it right straight to me."

Deborah wouldn't say a word after these remarks. Mary Jack increased the dose which did not take effect. Then she walked up to Deborah, turned her around, looked her in the eyes and said:

"Look here, you bitch, I'm talking to you."

Deborah was a very mild young girl. "I beg your pardon," she answered. "What were you saying?"

"You heard me. You know just what I'm saying. If you don't leave my man alone I'm going to cut you to ribbons. He only wants you for what you can give him. Don't let those pretty looks fool you. I'll mess them up plenty."

"He told me he was through with you," Deborah said tamely. "I guess it is your hustling money he gives me."

Everybody who was watching was tense and quiet. As quick as a flash Mary Jack threw her drink direct into Deborah's face, who threw hers back just as quick. They grabbed each other and started struggling and waltzing and tussling around the floor until they were separated. When Mary Jack adjusted her clothes and reached the door she stopped.

"Bitch," she said. "I'll wait for you outside."

"O.K., bitch," the timid little Deborah said.

The corner was crowded with people waiting to see just what was going to happen. A half hour later Deborah came out. As soon as she hit the sidewalk Mary Jack whipped out a bylow, a big knife with a large blade. She leapt upon Deborah and started cutting up and down her face. Deborah pulled the same kind of knife and went to work on Mary Jack the Bear. The crowd was terrified and did not dare to go near them. Every blow was aimed for the face, and every time one would slash the other, the crowd could go "Huh, my gawd!" They were both streaming with blood when they fell to the sidewalk exhausted, half an hour later.

The ambulance finally came and brought them both to the Charity Hospital. Mary Jack the Bear died later, but Deborah is still living. But her face is marked up so badly that it looks like a score board. The quarter has never forgotten that fight, one of the bloodiest anyone had ever seen.

Another bad woman who used to hang around the tonks in those days wore a full wig to hide her hair which was shorter than a man's. She met her Waterloo when she jumped an easy-going newcomer whom she tried to bully. They soon got into a hair-pulling fight, and her wig was pulled off and thrown to the floor. The roars of laughter that greeted this were more than she could take. She never bothered the newcomer afterwards. Several years later I learned that she had joined the church and left all the rough life behind her.

Other characters who had me spellbound in the third ward during those years were Black Benny, Cocaine Buddy, Nicodemus, Slippers, Red Cornelius, Aaron Harris and George Bo'hog. They were as tough as they come.

Nicodemus was a good gambler and one of the best dancers the honky-tonks had ever seen. He was a homely, liver-lipped sort of guy with a peculiar jazzy way of dancing and mugging that would send the gang in the tonk at Gravier and Franklin absolutely wild. When he got tired of playing cotch in the room at the back of the tonk he would come out on the dance floor and tell us to strike up a tune. And he would grab the sharpest chick standing by and would go into his two-step routine, swinging all around the place. The court house, parish prison, police station and the morgue were located across the street from the tonk. After midnight judges, lawyers and cops would make a beeline over to see Nicodemus dance. They always threw him a lot of money. Then he would go into the back room and gamble again.

Nicodemus had an awful temper and he would fight at the drop of a hat. He was jet black, a good man with the big knife called the chib, and most of the hustlers were afraid of him — except Black Benny.

Benny was really a different character from any of the would-be bad men I knew. He was a good bass drum beater in the brass bands, and he was very good at the trap drums also. Trap drums was the expression used in the early days for both the traps and the bass drums when the drummer in the tail gate bands played snare and bass at the same time. Benny was great, one of the best drummers we had in New Orleans.

Benny was the musician's friend. Whenever one of us was in hard luck Benny would help him out, and he was always ready to come to the aid of the underdog. Once when he was driving his coal wagon — he worked for Andrews as I did — he saw some big fellows sapping up a group of little kids. He jumped off his wagon at once and really made a stew of the bullies. Another time he had a fight with some firemen. He would have cleaned them up if one of them had not sneaked up behind him with a wagon shaft and knocked him cold. That was the only way Benny could be subdued.

When I was in my teens Benny was about twenty-six, a handsome fellow with smooth black skin, a strong body and a warm heart. He would not bother anyone, but God help the guy who tried to put anything over on him. One night he went into the back room of the honky-tonk to do a little gambling. In some way or other he and Nicodemus got into an argument over a bet. Nicodemus did not have his big knife, and Black Benny did not have anything on him either. In the heat of the argument Nicodemus jumped up from the table and rushed out to run home for his pistol. Everybody was telling Black Benny to cut out before Nicodemus came back.

"The hell with him," Benny said. "I ain't paying him any attention at all."

Instead of going home to get his pistol as Nicodemus had done Benny went out in a little alley beside the tonk to wait until Nicodemus came back with his big gun. While he was in the alley he stumbled on a piece of lead pipe about four feet long and as wide around as a Bologna sausage. The minute Benny's hand touched this pipe, he was satisfied that this was what he needed to give Nico a big surprise. Nico rushed down the alley and was about to enter the tonk when Benny swung on him with the lead pipe and knocked old Nico out cold.

There is one thing to be said about the fights between the bad men in my days. There was no malice and there was no dirty work. Let the best man win, that was the rule.

The gang loved both Benny and Nico. As soon as Nico had been knocked out the boys in the back room took the gun out of his pocket and hid it so that the cops would not know he had had it on him when he was hit. When the cops arrived they looked high and low for that gun but they could not find it. That's what I call sticking together. We did not want the cops to mix up in our quarrels; we could settle them ourselves.

Nicodemus never could get rid of the awful scar he received from that blasting on the side of his jaw given with all of Black Benny's strength. It was still with him when I saw him years later working in a well-known tavern in Calumet City near Chicago.

Even as a kid I thought Black Benny was the best bass drum beater I ever saw with any of the brass bands that ever set foot on New Orleans soil. I still say that he was one of the best all-around drummers that ever paraded in that city.

The cops knew Benny well, and they liked him so much they never beat him up the way they did the other guys they arrested. When Benny was serving time in jail the captain of the Parish Prison would let him out to play at funerals with our brass band. When the funeral was over he went back to prison just as though nothing had happened. This went on for years, but Benny never served more than thirty days at a stretch.

He was never in jail for stealing. It was always for some minor offense such as disturbing the peace, fighting or beating the hell out of his old lady Nelly. When he was not in jail for fighting, he would be in the hospital recovering from a carving she had given him.

Nelly was as tough as they make them. She was a small, good-looking, light-skinned colored girl who was not afraid of anybody, and when she and Benny got mixed up in a fight they were like two buzz saws. One day Benny was playing in the brass band in a street parade. Evidently he and Nelly had had a quarrel before he left home in the morning. The minute the parade swung down our street they spied each other at once and began calling each other names. And what names they were! I don't think they could even spell the words they used. Black Benny stopped immediately and took his bass drum off the strap which held it around his neck. Nelly started to cross the stone slab that served as a bridge across the gutter filled with muddy rain water. As Benny ran toward Nelly to beat her up he saw the stone slab. He picked it up and as Nelly ducked he let it fall in the middle of her back.

No one thought Nelly would ever get up again. They did not know Nelly. She started up at once, pulling her bylow knife out of her stocking and calling Benny all the black so and so's she could think of. He started to run, but he could not get away until she had sliced his ass plenty. They both ended up in the hospital. When they were released they went home to-

[79]

gether, smiling at each other as though nothing had happened.

It was about that time that Mama Lucy drifted away to some town in Florida. A large saw mill down there was taking on a lot of hands to fill the orders that were piling up. They were short on workers, and they had put an ad in the New Orleans *Item*, a paper I used to deliver. Workers on ordinary jobs could make a lot more money in Florida than they could in New Orleans, and Mama Lucy was among the hundreds of people who went. She stayed in Florida a long time and I began to think I would never see my dear sister again.

When Mama Lucy left, she and our cousin Flora Miles had become large teen-agers. Since the two of them ran around together most of the time Flora was left pretty much alone. Then she began to go around with another bunch of teen-agers who did not have the experience which Flora and Mama Lucy had had. Both of them had lived in the heart of the honky-tonk quarter; they knew the people who hung around them all the time; they had seen a good deal of fast life; and they were hard to fool. They were a little more jive proof than the average teen-ager, and they did practically everything they wanted to without their parents' knowing anything about it.

While Flora was going around with those strange kids she got into trouble. Through an old white fellow who used to have those colored girls up to an old ramshackle house of his. I do not need to tell you what he was up to.

My cousin Flora Miles became pregnant. I was just a youngster and neither I nor any of the rest of us knew what to do about the problem. All I could do was to watch Flora get larger and larger until a fine little fat baby arrived. Flora named him Clarence. When the girls in Flora's crowd realized what had happened to her as well as to a couple of other kids, they were scared to death and began to stay at home with their parents.

Everybody told old man Ike Miles, Flora's father, to have that old man arrested. But that did not make sense. He was a white man. If we had tried to have him arrested the judge would have had us all thrown out in the street, including baby Clarence. We put that idea out of our minds and did the next best thing. There was only one thing to do and that was a job for me. I had to take care of Clarence myself and, believe me, it was really a struggle.

My whole family had always been poor, and when Clarence was born I was the only one making a pretty decent salary. That was no fortune, but I was doing lots better than the rest of us. I was selling papers and playing a little music on the side. When things got rough I would go out to Front o' Town where there were a lot of produce houses. They sorted lots of potatoes, onions, cabbage, chickens, turkeys — in fact, all kinds of food to be sold to the big hotels and restaurants.

The spoiled products were thrown into big barrels which were left on the sidewalk for the garbage wagons to take away. Before they came I dug into the barrels and pulled out the best things I could find, such as half-spoiled chickens, turkeys, ducks, geese, and so on. At home we would cut out the bad parts, boil the good parts thoroughly, dress them nicely and put them in a basket. They looked very tasty and we sold them to the fine restaurants for whatever the proprietor wanted to pay. Usually we were given a good price with a few sandwiches and a good meal thrown in. We did the same thing with potatoes, cutting out the bad parts and selling the good parts for six-bits a sack. Naturally they paid more for the fowls.

We thought we had cleaned out everything that could possibly be used from those garbage barrels at the produce houses, but when the garbage wagons arrived at the Silver City dump a lot of poor colored people were waiting for them with pokers in their hands to pick out the good garbage from the bad. Sometimes they would find whole pork chops, unspoiled loaves of bread, clothing and other things that were useful. Sometimes I followed the wagons out to the dump myself hoping to find other things worth keeping or selling. This is one of the ways I helped the family raise the new-born baby Clarence.

As the years rolled by, I became very much attached to Clarence. Flora must have felt that she was going to die for just before she passed away she made his name Clarence Armstrong and left him in my care. Clarence became very much attached to me also. He had a very cute smile and I would spend many hours playing with him.

When she died Flora was living with my cousin Sarah Ann, her sister, a very jolly young lady with a big heart who did everything in her power to make people happy. She and my mother were running mates, and they would go places together, places where we kids did not dare poke our heads.

Flora had been in trouble ever since Clarence was born. The very day of his birth there was a terrible storm, one of the worst New Orleans had ever had. Houses were blown down, people and animals were killed, and thousands were homeless.

The storm broke with great suddenness when I was in the street on my way home. The wind blew so hard that slates were torn off the roof tops and thrown into the streets. I should have taken refuge, for the slates were falling all around me and I might have been killed as a number of other people were.

When I finally reached home I was soaking wet and exhausted. Mayann and Sara Ann were scared to death for fear I might have been killed in the storm. I had been real frantic while I was struggling to get home for fear the wind had blown my house and family off into some strange neighborhood. When I came in I threw my arms around mother and Sarah Ann, and while I was hugging them I looked at our only bed, in which mother, sister and I slept. There I saw the baby Clarence, and it took all the gloom out of me.

The next day the sun came out real pretty and bright, and everyone was smiling. All over the city, however, casualties were high, and there were lots of funerals that week. Joe Oliver, Bunk Johnson, Freddie Keppard and Henry Allen, all of whom played trumpets in brass bands, made a lot of money playing at funerals for lodge members who had been killed in the storm.

I am sure that the birth of Clarence and the shock of the storm had something to do with Flora's death. In the South, especially in those days, it was not easy to get a doctor, and it was a damn sight harder to get the money to pay for him. We could not afford a doctor at two dollars a visit; we needed that money to eat. Of course we did everything we could to help Flora, but we could not do enough. The Charity Hospital was filled to overflowing and patients had to be left in the yard.

Mama Lucy, who was still young, came back from Florida to help at Flora's funeral. She did everything she could to help us with food and other essentials, but she had not brought much money back with her. In Florida she was doing common labor and that does not pay much. Nobody in my family had a trade, and we all had to make a living as day laborers. As far back as I can see up our family tree there isn't a soul who knew anything that had to be learned at a school.

My Life in New Orleans

Mama Lucy and Sarah Ann both had a great sense of humor, and I loved them both. The three of us struggled together pretty near all our lives, but despite our hardships I would gladly live it all over again. With fifteen cents Mayann could make the finest dishes you would ever want to eat. When she sent me to the Poydras Market to get fifteen cents' worth of fish heads she made a big pot of "cubie yon" which she served with tomato sauce and fluffy white rice with every grain separate. We almost made ourselves sick eating this dish.

I thought her creole gumbo was the finest in the world. Her cabbage and rice was marvelous. As for red beans and rice, well, I don't have to say anything about that. It is my birth mark.

Mayann taught us both how to cook her best dishes. Her jumbalaya was delicious. It is a concoction of diced Bologna sausage, shrimp, oysters, hard-shell crabs mixed with rice and flavored with tomato sauce. If you ever tasted Mayann's jumbalaya and did not lick your fingers my name is not Louis Satchmo Daniel Armstrong.

Speaking of food reminds me of the time I worked as a dish washer in Thompson's restaurant at Canal and Rampart Streets. I was permitted to eat all the cream puffs, doughnuts and ice cream I wanted. That was fine for two weeks, but after that I became so tired of those foods that the very sight of them nauseated me. So I quit and went back to my old job in Andrews Coal

Yard. That was when I wrote *Coal Cart Blues,* which I recorded years later.

I was glad to get back to this job again, playing from time to time for dances, picnics, funerals and an occasional street parade on Sundays. My salary was pretty good. Real good I'd say for a youngster my age. I still got a thrill out of working in the coal yards with the old hustlers. At lunch time I would sit with them with my ten-cent mug of beer and my poor boy sandwich. Most of the time I would just listen, but when I threw in my two cents' worth the idea they would even listen to me just thrilled me all over.

Ever since I was a small kid I have always been a great observer. I had noticed that the boys I ran with had prostitutes working for them. They did not get much money from their gals, but they got a good deal of notoriety. I wanted to be in the swim so I cut in on a chick. She was not much to look at, but she made good money, or what in those days I thought was big money. I was a green inexperienced kid as far as women were concerned, particularly when one of them was walking the streets for me. She was short and nappy haired and she had buck teeth. Of course I am not trying to ridicule her; what counts is the woman herself, not her looks. I did not take her seriously, nor any other woman for that matter. I have always been wrapped up in my music and no woman in the world can change that. Right until this day my horn comes first.

She had the nerve to be jealous, but I did not pay

any attention. One day she wanted me to go home and spend the night with her.

"I wouldn't think of staying away from Mayann and Mama Lucy," I said, "not even for one night. I have never done it before and I won't do it now. Mayann and Mama Lucy are not used to that."

"Aw, hell," she said. "You are a big boy now. Come on and stay."

"No."

Before I realized what she was doing she pulled her knife on me. It was not the kind of large knife Mary Jack the Bear or Deborah carried, it was a pocket knife. She stabbed me in the left shoulder and the blood ran down over the back of my shirt.

I was afraid to tell Mayann about it, but she found out about it at once when she saw the blood on my shirt. At the sight of the blood she got mad.

"Who did it? Who did it?" she asked, shaking me.

"Er . . . my chick did."

"Oh! *She* did it! "

"Yes."

"What right has she cutting on you? "

With fear in my eyes, I told her the whole story. Mayann would not stand for foolishness from me or anybody else. The minute I told what happened she pushed me aside and made a beeline to my chick's house.

The girl was just about ready to go to bed when

Mayann banged on her door. The minute she opened the door Mayann grabbed her by the throat.

"What you stab my son for?"

Before she could say one word Mayann threw her on the floor and began choking her to death. Mayann was a big, strong woman and she would have killed her if it had not been for Black Benny and some of the boys who gambled and rushed the growler around Liberty and Perdido. Benny knew Mayann well, and he and I had played quite a few funerals together.

"Don't kill her, Mayann," Benny shouted when he rushed in. "She won't do it again."

Mayann kind of let up.

"Don't ever bother my boy again," she said. "You are too old for him. He did not want to hurt your feelings, but he don't want no more of you."

She was right. After I discovered my chick was just as tough as Mary Jack the Bear, I was afraid of her.

chapter 6

ARTHUR BROWN was one of my playmates at school.
He was a quiet good-looking youngster with nice manners and a way of treating the girls that made them go
wild about him. I admired the way he played it cool.
He was going with a girl who had a little brother who
was very cute. Too cute, I would say, since he was always playing with a pistol or a knife. We did not pay
much attention to the kid, but one day when he was
cleaning his gun he pointed it at Arthur Brown saying
"I am going to shoot." Sure enough, he pulled the
trigger; the gun was loaded and Arthur Brown fell to
the ground with a bullet in his head.

It was a terrible shock. We all felt so bad that even the boys cried.

When Arthur was buried we all chipped in and hired a brass band to play at his funeral. Beautiful girls Arthur used to go with came to the funeral from all over the city, from Uptown, Downtown, Front o' Town and Back o' Town. Every one of them was weeping. We kids, all of us teen-agers, were pall bearers. The band we hired was the finest I had ever heard. It was the Onward Brass Band with Joe "King" Oliver and Emmanuel Perez blowing the cornets. Big tall Eddy Jackson booted the bass tuba. A bad tuba player in a brass band can make work hard for the other musicians, but Eddy Jackson knew how to play that tuba and he was the ideal man for the Onward Brass Band. Best of all was Black Benny playing the bass drum. The world really missed something by not digging Black Benny on that bass drum before he was killed by a prostitute.

It was a real sad moment when the Onward Brass Band struck up the funeral march as Arthur Brown's body was being brought from the church to the graveyard. Everybody cried, including me. Black Benny beat the bass drum with a soft touch, and Babe Mathews put a handkerchief under his snare to deaden the tone. *Nearer My God to Thee* was played as the coffin was lowered into the grave.

As pallbearers Cocaine Buddy, Little Head Lucas, Egg Head Papa, Harry Tennisen and myself wore the darkest clothes we had, blue suits for the most part. Later that same year Harry Tennisen was killed by a hustling gal of the honky-tonks called Sister Pop. Her pimp was named Pop and was well known as a good cotch player. Pop did not know anything about the affair until Sister Pop shot Harry in the brain with a big forty-five gun and killed him instantly. Later on Lucas and Cocaine Buddy died natural deaths of T.B.

The funerals in New Orleans are sad until the body is finally lowered into the grave and the Reverend says, "ashes to ashes and dust to dust." After the brother was six feet under ground the band would strike up one of those good old tunes like *Didn't He Ramble,* and all the people would leave their worries behind. Particularly when King Oliver blew that last chorus in high register.

Once the band starts, everybody starts swaying from one side of the street to the other, especially those who drop in and follow the ones who have been to the funeral. These people are known as "the second line" and they may be anyone passing along the street who wants to hear the music. The spirit hits them and they follow along to see what's happening. Some follow only a few blocks, but others follow the band until the whole affair is over.

Wakes are usually held when the body is laid out in the house or the funeral parlor. The family of the deceased usually serves a lot of coffee, cheese and crackers all night long so that the people who come to sing hymns over the corpse can eat and drink to their heart's delight. I used to go to a lot of wakes and lead off with a hymn. After everybody had joined in the chorus I would tiptoe on into the kitchen and load up on crackers, cheese and coffee. That meal always tasted specially good. Maybe it was because that meal was a freebie and didn't cost me anything but a song — or I should say, a hymn.

There was one guy who went to every wake in town. It did not matter whose wake it was. In some way he would find out about it and get there, rain or shine, and lead off with a hymn. When I got old enough to play in the brass band with good old-timers like Joe Oliver, Roy Palmer, Sam Dutrey and his brother Honore, Oscar Celestin, Oak Gasper, Buddy Petit, Kid Ory and Mutt Carey and his brother Jack I began noticing this character more frequently. Once I saw him in church looking very sad and as if he was going to cry any minute. His clothes were not very good and his pants and coat did not match. What I admired about him was that he managed to look very presentable. His clothes were well pressed and his shoes shined. Finally I found out the guy was called Sweet Child.

For some time funerals gave me the only chance I had to blow my cornet. The war had started, and all the dance halls and theaters in New Orleans had been closed down. A draft law had been passed and everybody had to work or fight. I was perfectly willing to go into the Army, but they were only drafting from the age of twenty-one to twenty-five and I was only seventeen. I tried to get into the Navy, but they checked up on my birth certificate and threw me out. I kept up my hope and at one enlistment office a soldier told me to come back in a year. He said that if the war was still going on I could capture the Kaiser and win a great, big prize. "Wouldn't that be swell," I thought. "Capture the Kaiser and win the war." Believe me, I lived to see that day.

Since I did not have a chance to play my cornet, I did odd jobs of all kinds. For a time I worked unloading the banana boats until a big rat jumped out of a bunch I was carrying to the checker. I dropped that bunch and started to run. The checker hollered at me to come back and get my time, but I didn't stop running until I got home. Since then bananas have terrified me. I would not eat one if I was starving. Yet I can remember how I used to love them. I could eat a whole small ripe bunch all by myself when the checker could not see me.

Every time things went bad with me I had the coal cart to fall back on, thanks to my good stepfather Gabe. I sure did like him, and I used to tease Mayann about it.

"Mama, you know one thing?" I would say. "Papa Gabe is the best step-pa I've ever had. He is the best out of the whole lot of them."

Mayann would kind of chuckle and say:

"Aw, go on, you Fatty O'Butler."

That was the time when the moving picture actor Fatty Arbuckle was in his prime and very popular in New Orleans. Mayann never did get his name right. It sounded so good to me when she called me Fatty O'Butler that I never told her different.

I would stay at the coal yard with father Gabe until I thought I had found something better, that is something that was easier. It was hard work shoveling coal and sitting behind my mule all day long, and I used to get awful pains in my back. So any time I could find a hustle that was just a little lighter, I would run to it like a man being chased.

The job I took with Morris Karnoffsky was easier, and I stayed with him a long time. His wagon went through the red-light district, or Storyville, selling stone coal at a nickel a bucket. Stone coal was what they called hard coal. One of the reasons I kept the job with Morris Karnoffsky was that it gave me a chance to go through Storyville in short pants. Since I was working with a man, the cops did not bother me. Otherwise they would have tanned my hide if they had caught me rambling around that district. They were very strict with us youngsters and I don't blame them. The temptation was great and weakminded kids could have sure messed things up.

As for me I was pretty wise to things. I had been brought up around the honky-tonks on Liberty and Perdido where life was just about the same as it was in Storyville except that the chippies were cheaper. The gals in my neighborhood did not stand in cribs wearing their fine silk lingerie as they did in Storyville. They wore the silk lingerie just the same, but under their regular clothes. Our hustlers sat on their steps and called to the "Johns" as they passed by. They had to keep an eye on the cops all the time, because they weren't allowed to call the tricks like the girls in Storyville. That was strictly a business center. Music, food and everything else was good there.

All of the cribs had a small fireplace. When our wagon passed by, the girls would holler out to Morris and tell him to have his boy bring in some coal. I would bring them whatever they ordered, and they would generally ask me to start a fire for them or put some coal on the fire that was already burning. While I was fixing the fire I couldn't help stealing a look at them, which always sent me into a cold sweat. I did not dare say anything, but I had eyes, and very good ones at the time, and I used them. It seemed to me that some of the beautiful young women I saw standing in those doorways should have been home with their parents.

What I appreciated most about being able to go into Storyville without being bothered by the cops, was Pete Lala's cabaret where Joe Oliver had his band and where he was blowing up a storm on his cornet. Nobody could touch him. Harry Zeno, the best known drummer in New Orleans, was playing with him at the time. What I admired most about Zeno was that no matter how hard he played the sporting racket he never

[95]

let it interfere with his profession. And that's something the modern day musician has to learn. Nothing ever came between Harry Zeno and his drums.

There were other members of Joe Oliver's band whose names have become legendary in music. The world will never be able to replace them, and I say that from the bottom of my heart. These musicians were Buddy Christian, guitar (he doubled on piano also); Zue Robertson, trombone; Jimmy Noone, clarinet; Bob Lyons, bass violin; and last but not least Joe Oliver on the cornet. That was the hottest jazz band ever heard in New Orleans between the years 1910 and 1917.

Harry Zeno died in the early part of 1917 and his funeral was the largest ever held for any musician. Sweet Child, by the way, was at this funeral too, singing away as though he was a member of Zeno's lodge. The Onward Brass Band put him away with those fine, soothing funeral marches.

Not long after Zeno died talk started about closing down Storyville. Some sailors on leave got mixed up in a fight and two of them were killed. The Navy started a war on Storyville, and even as a boy I could see that the end was near. The police began to raid all the houses and cabarets. All the pimps and gamblers who hung around a place called Twenty-Five while their chicks were working were locked up.

It sure was a sad scene to watch the law run all those people out of Storyville. They reminded me of a gang of refugees. Some of them had spent the best part of their lives there. Others had never known any other kind of life. I have never seen such weeping and carrying-on. Most of the pimps had to go to work or go to jail, except a privileged few.

A new generation was about to take over in Storyville. My little crowd had begun to look forward to other kicks, like our jazz band, our quartet and other musical activities.

Joe Lindsey and I formed a little orchestra. Joe was a very good drummer, and Morris French was a good man on the trombone. He was a little shy at first, but we soon helped him to get over that. Another shy lad was Louis Prevost who played the clarinet, but how he could play once he got started! We did not use a piano in those days. There were only six pieces: cornet, clarinet, trombone, drums, bass violin and guitar, and when those six kids started to swing, you would swear it was Ory and Oliver's jazz band.

Kid Ory and Joe Oliver got together and made one of the hottest jazz bands that ever hit New Orleans. They often played in a tail gate wagon to advertise a ball or other entertainments. When they found themselves on a street corner next to another band in another wagon, Joe and Kid Ory would shoot the works. They would give with all that good mad music they had under their belts and the crowd would go wild. When the other band decided it was best to cut the competition and start out for another corner, Kid Ory played a little tune on his trombone that made the crowd go wild again. But this time they were wild with laughter. If you ever run into Kid Ory, maybe he will tell you the name of that tune. I don't dare write it here. It was a cute little tune to celebrate the defeat of the enemy. I thought it screamingly funny and I think you would too.

Kid knew how much Joe Oliver cared for me. He also knew that, great as he was, Joe Oliver would never do anything that would make me look small in the eyes of the public. Oftentimes when our band was on the street advertising a lawn party or some other entertainment, our tail wagon would run into the Ory-Oliver's band. When this happened Joe had told me to stand up so that he would be sure to see me and not do any carving. After he saw me he would stand up in his wagon, play a few short pieces and set out in another direction.

One day when we were advertising for a ball we ran into Oliver and his band. I was not feeling very well that day and I forgot to stand up. What a licking those guys gave us. Sure enough when our wagon started to leave, Kid Ory started to play that get-away tune at us. The crowd went mad. We felt terrible about it, but we took it like good sports because there was not any other band that could do that to us. We youngsters were the closest rivals the Ory band had.

I saw Joe Oliver the night of the day he had cut in on us.

"Why in hell," he said before I could open my mouth, "didn't you stand up?"

"Papa Joe, it was all my fault. I promise I won't ever do that again."

We laughed it all off, and Joe brought me a bottle of beer. This was a feather in my cap because Papa Joe was a safe man, and he did not waste a lot of money buying anybody drinks. But for me he would do anything he thought would make me happy.

At that time I did not know the other great musicians such as Jelly Roll Morton, Freddy Keppard, Jimmy Powlow, Bab Frank, Bill Johnson, Sugar Johnny, Tony Jackson, George Fields and Eddy Atkins. All of them had left New Orleans long before the red-light district was closed by the Navy and the law. Of course I met most of them in later years, but Papa Joe Oliver, God bless him, was my man. I often did errands for Stella Oliver, his wife, and Joe would give me lessons for my pay. I could not have asked for anything I wanted more. It was my ambition to play as he did. I still think that if it had not been for Joe Oliver jazz would not be what it is today. He was a creator in his own right.

Mrs. Oliver also became attached to me, and treated me as if I were her own son. She had a little girl by her first marriage named Ruby, whom I knew when she was just a little shaver. She is married now and has a daughter who will be married soon.

One of the nicest things Joe Oliver did for me

when I was a youngster was to give me a beat-up old cornet of his which he had blown for years. I prized that horn and guarded it with my life. I blew on it for a long, long time before I was fortunate enough to get another one.

Cornets were much cheaper then than they are today, but at that they cost sixty-five dollars. You had to be a big shot musician making plenty of money to pay that price for a horn. I remember how such first rate musicians as Hamp Benson, Kid Ory, Zoo French, George Brashere, Joe Petit and lots of other fellows I played with beamed all over when they got new horns. They acted just as though they had received a brand new Cadillac.

I got my first brand new cornet on the installment plan with "a little bit down" and a "little bit now and then." Whenever my collector would catch up with me and start talking about a "little bit now" I would tell him:

"I'll give you-all a little bit *then*, but I'm damned if I can give you-all a little bit *now*."

Cornet players used to pawn their instruments when there was a lull in funerals, parades, dances, gigs and picnics. Several times I went to the pawnshop and picked up some loot on my horn. Once it was to play cotch and be around the good old hustlers and gamblers.

I can never stop loving Joe Oliver. He was always ready to come to my rescue when I needed someone to tell me about life and its little intricate things, and help me out of difficult situations. That is what happened when I met a gal named Irene, who had just arrived from Memphis, Tennessee, and did not know a soul in New Orleans. She got mixed up with a gambler in my neighborhood named Cheeky Black who gave her a real hard time. She used to come into a honky-tonk where I was playing with a three piece combo. I played the cornet; Boogus, the piano; and Sonny Garbie, the drums. After their night's work was over, all the hustling gals used to come into the joint around four or five o'clock in the morning. They would ask us to beat out those fine blues for them and buy us drinks, cigarettes, or anything we wanted.

I noticed that everyone was having a good time except Irene. One morning during an intermission I went over to talk to her and she told me her whole story. Cheeky Black had taken every nickel she had earned and she had not eaten for two days. She was as raggedy as a bowl of slaw. That is where I came in with my soft heart. I was making a dollar and twenty-five cents a night. That was a big salary in those days — if I got it; some nights they paid us, and some nights they didn't. Anyway I gave Irene most of my salary until she could get on her feet.

That went on until she and Cheeky Black came to the parting of the ways. There was only one thing Irene could do: take refuge under my wing. I had not had any experience with women, and she taught me all I know.

We fell deeply in love. My mother did not know this at first. When she did find out, being the great little trouper she was, she made no objections. She felt that I was old enough to live my own life and to think for myself. Irene and I lived together as man and wife. Then one fine day she was taken deathly sick. As she had been very much weakened by the dissipated life she had led her body could not resist the sickness that attacked her. Poor girl! She was twenty-one, and I was just turning seventeen. I was at a loss as to what to do for her.

The worst was when she began to suffer from stomach trouble. Every night she groaned so terribly that she was nearly driving me crazy. I was desperate when I met my fairy godfather, Joe Oliver. I ran into him when I was on my way to Poydras Market to get some fish heads to make a cubie yon for Irene the way Mayann had taught me how to cook it. Papa Joe was on his way to play for a funeral.

"Hello, kid. What's cooking?" he asked.

"Nothing," I said sadly.

Then I told him about Irene's sickness and how much I loved her.

"You need money for a doctor? Is that it?" he said immediately. "Go down and take my place at Pete Lala's for two nights."

He was making top money down there — a dollar

and a half a night. In two nights I would make enough money to engage a very good doctor and get Irene's stomach straightened out. I was certainly glad to make the money I needed so much, and I was also glad to have a chance to blow my cornet again. It had been some time since I had used it.

"Papa Joe," I said, "I appreciate your kindness, but I do not think I am capable of taking your place."

Joe thought for a moment and then he said:

"Aw, go'wan and play in my place. If Pete Lala says anything to you tell him I sent ya."

As bad as I actually needed the money I was scared to death. Joe was such a powerful figure in the district that Pete Lala was not going to accept a nobody in his place. I could imagine him telling me so in these very words.

When I went there the next night, out of the corner of my eye I could see Pete coming before I had even opened my cornet case. I dumbed up and took my place on the bandstand.

"Where's Joe?" Pete asked.

"He sent me to work in his place," I answered nervously.

To my surprise Pete Lala let me play that night. However, every five minutes he would drag his club foot up to the bandstand in the very back of the cabaret.

"Boy," he would say, "put that bute in your horn."

I could not figure what on earth he was talking about until the end of the evening when I realized he meant to keep the mute in. When the night was over he told me that I did not need to come back.

I told Papa Joe what had happened and he paid me for the two nights anyway. He knew how much I needed the money, and besides that was the way he acted with someone he really liked.

Joe quit Pete Lala's when the law began to close down Storyville on Saturday nights, the best night in the week. While he was looking for new fields he came to see Irene and me, and we cooked a big pot of good gumbo for him. Irene had gotten well, and we were happy again.

The year 1917 was a turning point for me. Joe Lindsey left the band. He had found a woman who made him quit playing with us. It seemed as though Joe did not have much to say about the matter; this woman had made up Joe's mind for him. In any case that little incident broke up our little band, and I did not see any more of the fellows for a long time, except when I occasionally ran into one of them at a gig. But my bosom pal Joe Lindsey was not among them.

When I did see Joe again he was a private chauffeur driving a big, high-powered car. Oh, he was real fancy! There was a good deal of talk about the way Joe had left the band and broken up our friendship to go off with that woman. I told them that Joe had not broken up our friendship, that we had been real true friends from childhood and that we would continue to be as long as we lived.

[104]

Everything had gone all right for Seefus, as we called Joe, so long as he was just a poor musician like the rest of us. But there's a good deal of truth in the old saying about all that glitters ain't gold. Seefus had a lot of bad luck with that woman of his. In the first place she was too old for him, much too old. I thought Irene was a little too old for me, but Seefus went me one better — he damn near tied up with an old grandma. And to top it off he married the woman. My God, did she give him a bad time! Soon after their marriage she dropped him like a hot potato. He suffered terribly from wounded vanity and tried to kill himself by slashing his throat with a razor blade. Seeing what had happened to Joe, I told Irene that since she was now going straight, she should get an older fellow. I was so wrapped up in my horn that I would not make a good mate for her. She liked my sincerity and she said she would always love me.

After that I went to the little town of Houma, La. — where the kid we called Houma, at the Home, came from — to play in a little band owned by an undertaker called Bonds. He was so nice to me that I stayed longer than I had planned. It was a long, long time before I saw Irene or Joe Lindsey, but I often thought about them both.

Things had not changed much when I returned to New Orleans. In my quarter I still continued to run across old lady Magg, who had raised almost all the kids in the neighborhood. Both she and Mrs. Martin, the school teacher, were old-timers in the district. So too was Mrs. Laura — we never bothered about a person's last name — whom I remember dearly. Whenever one of these three women gave any of us kids a spanking we did not go home and tell our parents because we would just get another one from them. Mrs. Magg, I am sure, is still living.

When I returned from Houma I had to tell Mrs. Magg everything that had happened during the few weeks I was there. Mr. Bonds paid me a weekly salary, and I had my meals at his home, which was his undertaking establishment. He had a nice wife and I sure did enjoy the way she cooked those fresh butter beans, the beans they call Lima beans up North. The most fun we had in Houma was when we played at one of the country dances. When the hall was only half full I used to have to stand and play my cornet out of the window. Then, sure enough, the crowd would come rolling in. That is the way I let the folks know for sure that a real dance was going on that night. Once the crowd was in, that little old band would swing up a breeze.

Being young and wild, whenever I got paid at the end of a week, I would make a beeline for the gambling house. In less than two hours I would be broker than the Ten Commandments. When I came back to Mayann she put one of her good meals under my belt, and I decided never to leave home again. No matter where I went, I always remembered Mayann's cooking.

One day some of the boys in the neighborhood thought up the fantastic idea to run away from home and hobo out to get a job on a sugar cane plantation. We rode a freight train as far as Harrihan, not over thirty miles from New Orleans. I began to get real hungry, and the hungrier I got the more I thought about those good meat balls and spaghetti Mayann was cooking the morning we left. I decided to give the whole thing up.

"Look here, fellows," I said. "I'm sorry, but this don't make sense. Why leave a good home and all that good cooking to roam around the country without money? I am going back to my mother on the next freight that passes."

And believe me, I did. When I got home Mayann did not even know that I had lit out for the cane fields.

"Son," she said, "you are just in time for supper."

I gave a big sigh of relief. Then I resolved again never to leave home unless Papa Joe Oliver sent for me. And I didn't either.

I don't want anyone to feel I'm posing as a plaster saint. Like everyone I have my faults, but I always have believed in making an honest living. I was determined to play my horn against all odds, and I had to sacrifice a whole lot of pleasure to do so. Many a night the boys in my neighborhood would go uptown to Mrs. Cole's lawn, where Kid Ory used to hold sway. The other boys were sharp as tacks in their fine suits of clothes.

I did not have the money they had and I could not dress as they did, so I put Kid Ory out of my mind. And Mayann, Mama Lucy and I would go to some nickel show and have a grand time.

chapter 7

I TOOK A LOT OF ODD JOBS to keep my head above water and to help out Mayann and Mama Lucy. For instance, I worked on a junk wagon with a fellow named Lorenzo. He was a very funny fellow and he did not pay me much, but the fun we used to have going all over the city to collect rags, bones and bottles from the rich as well as the poor!

Lorenzo had an old tin horn which he used to blow without the mouthpiece, and he could actually play a tune on it, and with feeling too. It was one of those long tin horns with a wooden mouthpiece which people used to buy to celebrate Christmas and New

Years. It used to knock me out to hear him play a real tune to call people out of their houses and back yards. In the junk people discarded there were sometimes nice things such as suits or clothes which occasionally fitted me like a glove. Once he bought a complete suit of clothes from some white people on Charles Street which he let me have for what he had paid for it. That wasn't very much and oh, was I sharp!

Satisfied that I had learned the business well, he would occasionally let me take the day's collection to the junk yard for the weigh-up. I liked that job. There was one thing I could not figure out about Lorenzo. With all the money he made he never got his teeth fixed. Every other tooth was missing, and he looked just like he was laughing twice as hard as anyone else when something funny was said. But I did not dare put him wise to this because I did not want older folks to think me a sassy child. I thought a lot of Lorenzo, and I would gladly live over those days with him again. When I was with him I was in my element. The things he said about music held me spellbound, and he blew that old, beat-up tin horn with such warmth that I felt as though I was sitting with a good cornet player.

A pie man named Santiago blew a bugle to attract customers as he walked down the street with his big basket of pies on his arm. He could swing it too, and so could the waffle man who drove around town in a big wagon fitted out with a kitchen. When he blew his mess call the customers came running, and when those hustling guys met him as they came home from gambling all night, they'd all but chain his wheels to keep him from leaving.

There were many different kinds of people and instruments to inspire me to carry on with my music when I was a boy. I always loved music, and it did not matter what the instrument was or who played it so long as the playing was good. I used to hear some of the finest music in the world listening to the barroom quartets who hung around the saloons with a cold can of beer in their hands, singing up a breeze while they passed the can around. I thought I was really somebody when I got so I could hang around with those fellows — sing and drink out of the can with them. When I was a teen-ager those old-timers let me sing with them and carry the lead, bless their hearts. Even in those days they thought I had something on the ball as a ragtime singer, which is what hot swing singing is today.

Black Benny used to be there on that street corner or the saloon when he wasn't busy gambling, playing music, or playing the girls. You should have heard his good old barroom tenor sing *Sweet Adeline* or *Mr. Jefferson Lord — Play that Barber-Shop Chord*. But you had to keep an eye on Benny when a can of beer was passed around. When a bunch of fellows got together the chances were that there wasn't more than a dime in the crowd. Naturally that dime went for a big tin bucket filled with ice cold beer. It was so cold that no one could take more than three swallows at most.

Except Black Benny. If anyone made the mistake of passing that growler to him first he would put it to his chops and all we could see was his Adam's apple moving up and down like a perpetual motion machine. We heard a regular google, google, google. Then he would take the can from his mouth with a sigh, wipe the foam off his mouth with his shirt sleeve and pass the can politely to the guy next to him as though it still had plenty of beer in it. Nay, nay, Black Benny with his asbestos throat had drunk every drop of that beer.

Black Benny had such a cute way about him that he could get away with nearly everything he did. Benny seldom had any money because the better gamblers kept him broke and in pawn. When he was lucky he would get his good clothes out of pawn and buy everyone in sight a drink. Then he would really rush the can. But everyone else drank first. We weren't taking any chances even if Benny had bought the beer. We figured Benny might act like the guy who brought a bag of oranges to a sick friend in the hospital and ate them all himself while he sat by the bedside.

When I came back from Houma things were much tougher. The Kaiser's monkey business was getting worse, and, what is more, a serious flu epidemic had hit New Orleans. Everybody was down with it, except me. That was because I was physic-minded. I never missed a week without a physic, and that kept all kinds of sickness out of me.

Just when the government was about to let crowds

of people congregate again so that we could play our horns once more the lid was clamped down tighter than ever. That forced me to take any odd jobs I could get. With everybody suffering from the flu, I had to work and play the doctor to everyone in my family as well as all my friends in the neighborhood. If I do say so, I did a good job curing them.

Finally I got work playing in a honky-tonk run by a white Italian guy named Henry Matranga. The law had not shut him down, as it had the places in Storyville, because his joint was third rate. There I could play a lot of blues for cheap prostitutes and hustlers. At least for a time, for eventually Matranga had to close down too.

Henry Matranga was as sharp as a tack and a playboy in his own right. He treated everybody fine, and the colored people who patronized his tonk loved him very much. My mother used to work at his home, just a few blocks away from his saloon, and I used to go to see her there. If I came at mealtime they would make me sit down in the kitchen to eat a plate of their good Italian spaghetti. That family always enjoyed seeing me eat.

Matranga did not bother much with his customers. Knowing how sensitive my people are when white folks shout orders at them and try to boss them around, he left it to Slippers, the bouncer, to keep order.

While I was there I saw some serious fights, such as the Saturday night gun battle between Slippers and

[113]

a guy from the swamps near the levee. Those workers were paid on Saturday night, got drunk and headed straight for town and the honky-tonk where I was playing. Slippers was a good man with his dukes. He did not bother anybody, but God help any guy who started anything with him or raised a row in Matranga's joint.

The night the fellow from the levee camp came in he lost all his money gambling in the back room. Slippers was watching him when he tried to stick everybody up and get his money back from the game keeper. Slippers tried to reason with him, but the guy kept on bellyaching. Finally Slippers picked him up by the seat of the pants and threw him out on the sidewalk. The fellows around the gambling table had forgotten to tell Slippers that the guy had a gun. While the door was being closed the guy pulled out a big .45 and fired three shots, but these shots went wild. Slippers was a fast man on the draw. He winged the guy in the leg, and he was carried off to the hospital and then to jail.

When this happened the three musicians in our band were scared to death. Our stand was near the door. When the trouble started Boogus, the pianist, turned white as a sheet, and Garbee, the drummer, with his thick lips, started to stammer.

"Wha, wha, wha . . . what's that?"

"Nothing," I said, though I was just as scared as he was.

As a matter of fact, nothing did happen. The wounded man was carted off to the hospital, and about four o'clock the gals started piling in from their night's work. They bought us drinks, and we started those good old blues. Soon everybody forgot the whole thing.

One thing I always admired about those bad men when I was a youngster in New Orleans is that they all liked good music. Slippers liked my way of playing so much that he himself suggested to Henry Matranga that I replace the cornet player who had just left. He was a pretty good man, and Matranga was a little in doubt about my ability to hold the job down. When I opened up, Slippers was in my corner cheering me on.

"Listen to that kid," he said to Matranga. "Just listen to that little son-of-a-bitch blow that quail!"

That is what Slippers called my cornet. He never changed it as long as I played at Matranga's. Sometimes when we would really start going to town while Slippers was out in the gambling room in the back, he would run out on the dance floor saying:

"Just listen to that little son-of-bitch blow that quail!"

Then he would look at me.

"Boy, if you keep on like that, you're gonna be the best quail blower in the world. Mark my words."

Coming from Slippers those words made me feel grand. He knew music and he didn't throw compliments around to everybody.

Slippers and Black Benny were the two best men in the neighborhood with their dukes. They were always ready for a fair fight. But if anybody tried to sneak up behind them and do some dirty work, brother, they would get what was coming to them. If they had to, they could fight dirty. One thing I admired about Slippers and Black Benny is that they never got into a scrap with each other.

There were two other honky-tonks about a block away from Matranga's, but we youngsters did not go to them very often because some really bad characters hung around them, particularly around Spanol's joint. The ambulance was forever backing up to the door to take some guy to the hospital. If it wasn't the ambulance it was the patrol wagon to haul off to the morgue someone who had been shot or cut to death. We kids nixed the joint. The other tonk was Savocas'. We had to go there for our pay when we had been working on the levee unloading banana boats. Sometimes we worked those big ships all day, sometimes all night. When we finished we would light out for Savocas' honky-tonk and line up on the sidewalk to get our pay. Afterwards many guys went inside to the gambling room and lost every nickel they had earned. I couldn't afford to do that because I was the sole support of May-ann, Mama Lucy and my adopted son, Clarence. I wanted to do my best to keep their jaws jumping.

Clarence loved buttermilk. When the buttermilk man came around hollering "But-ter-milk. But-ter-milk," Clarence would wake up and say: "Papa, there's the buttermilk man!"

Clarence was going on two, and he was a cute kid.

He became very much attached to me, and since I was a great admirer of kids we got on wonderfully together. He played an important part in my life.

Mrs. Laura kept the lunch wagon in front of Henry Matranga's honky-tonk. When the night lifers got full of liquor, which was much stronger than the present day juice, they would line up religiously before her counter and stuff themselves like pigs. We musicians used to eat on credit and pay at the end of the week. Mrs. Laura made a good deal of money, but her husband, who was much younger than she, used to waste it on other women. Mrs. Laura was not much on looks, but she was happy and that was all that mattered.

During this period of my life I worked for a time as a helper on a milk wagon for a driver who was a very fine white boy. He was very kind and he made my work as easy as possible. Our route covered the West End and the summer resorts at Spanish Fort, and we delivered our milk in the early hours of the morning. The roads were made of oyster shells which were ground down by the traffic into a firm road bed. One Sunday morning I jumped on the wagon after it had started. My foot missed the step and was caught under one of the wheels, which rolled over it and ground it into the sharp, broken bits of oyster shells. Since the wagon was heavily loaded the top of my big toe was torn wide open and tiny, sharp pieces of shell were driven into the wound. The pain was terrible, and the boss drove me to the Charity Hospital miles away in New Orleans.

I like to have died at the hospital when the pieces of shell were taken out one by one. When the doctors learned that the accident had happened on a milk wagon of the Cloverland Company they asked me if I was going to sue them for damages.

"No sir," I said. "I think too much of my boss for that. Besides it wasn't his fault."

When I came home with my bandaged foot, Mayann went into a natural faint. She would always pass out cold whenever anything happened to her son Louis. Of course everybody in the neighborhood tried to persuade her to sue the milk company but she refused.

"If my son says no, that's that," she said.

If I had sued I could have probably gotten five hundred dollars, but I was not thinking about money. I was thinking about getting well, and about the fact that it was not my boss' fault, and about how kind he had been to me. The toe got well and the boss gave me a present anyway.

The next week another kid who worked on another wagon had an accident which was not serious at all, not nearly so serious as mine. He was the smart aleck type, and he sued. If he got anything out of the company at all he was lucky. The lawyers take the best part of any settlement they get. That is typical of the South.

The kids who worked as helpers for the milk

wagons used to get paid off around ten o'clock on Friday morning. After that we would go around the corner from the dairy and start a big crap game. I had not received a dime as settlement for my accident, but I was certainly lucky in those crap games. I used to come home with my pockets loaded with all kinds of dough, and finally Mayann got scared.

"Boy, where in the name of the Lord did you get all that money?" she asked.

I had to confess to keep her from thinking I had stolen it. Then I got ready for the good whipping I was sure she would give me for gambling.

"Son," she said instead, "be careful about your gambling. You remember the hard time your pa and I had getting the judge to let you out of the Waifs' Home."

I said "yassum," and went down to Canal Street to buy mother, sister and Clarence some real sharp clothes. I even bought a pair of tailor-made short pants for myself. I did not have enough money to buy shoes so I just dressed up barefoot as usual. New pants and a new blouse were all that counted.

For a long time after my accident I stayed with the milk company. Finally business slowed up. My boss was laid off and so was I. I had a hard time finding anything to do until the government opened up a big job on Poland and Dauphine Streets. The government was so short of workers that it had to have thousands shipped in from Puerto Rico. What a sight those fellows were! Most of them had scarcely any clothes, and some of them were barefooted like the boys in my neighborhood. We were glad enough to work with them although they had the nerve to look down on us because we were colored. We ignored that and managed to get along with them fairly well.

I was rather proud of that big yellow button I wore for identification when I went in and out of the yard. You can imagine how tough things were when many well-known musicians had to work on that job. Among them was Kid Ory, a carpenter by trade and a good one at that. It was good to see him and a lot of the other boys, and it made me happy to be on that job with them. To my surprise I also ran into my teen-age pal, Joe Lindsey. We were as happy to be together again as we were when we played in the little band together. At lunchtime we used to sit together on the logs they fed the pile driver, and talk endlessly. He told me about that woman he had left our little band to go to live with, and how she had finally left him for an older and more experienced man. That pretty near ruined him.

I told him all about Irene and me and about the sensible way in which we had parted. She had gone back to Cheeky Black and had not told me anything about it. Joe had a good laugh when I told him how I found it out.

After I returned from Houma I ran into Irene

one day and she asked me out to her place. I was careful to ask her if she had anybody else.

"Oh, no. Nobody," she said.

So I felt perfectly safe to go up to her room. We were just about to doze off to sleep when I heard the door knob rattle. Irene nearly jumped out of her skin.

"Who is it?" she asked.

I did not pay much attention, thinking it was merely a passing acquaintance. The door knob started to rattle again.

"Who is there?" she asked in a louder voice.

"It's Cheeky Black."

Then I began to think fast. Cheeky was a tough character. In those days when a chick said she had company, the caller outside was supposed to go away. Nothing of the sort happened. I had locked the door carefully myself, but Cheeky threw himself against it and it flew open as though there were no lock at all.

When Cheeky rushed in waving his razor Irene jumped out of bed screaming. She dodged past Cheeky and ran shrieking into the street with scarcely a stitch on. Cheeky was hot on her tail swinging that razor. Outside I could hear Irene's screams and the voices of people trying to pacify Cheeky and crying, "Don't cut her. Don't cut her."

While this was going on I was struggling to get into my clothes and get out of there as fast as I could. There was only one thought in my mind: Cheeky Black. What would happen to me if he came back? Finally

[121]

I managed to get enough clothes on so that I could run all the way back home to Mayann. When I rushed in all out of breath she said:

"Uh-huh! So you've been in another man's house with his old lady? This will teach you a lesson, won't it?"

"Believe me, I'll never do it again, mother."

Mayann laughed herself sick. She was not afraid of a living soul, and she told me not to worry. She would straighten things out with Cheeky Black. After all, I was innocent. Irene had no business asking me to her house while she was still living with Cheeky Black.

After Joe Lindsey had a good laugh over this story, I told him that if I never saw Irene again it would be too soon. As a matter of fact I never have.

When the government work was over I got a pretty good job with a wrecking company tearing down old houses. The amusing thing about that work is that you always have the hope that you will find some treasure that was hidden in the house years ago and forgotten. The boys I worked with told me they had had all kinds of luck in finding money and jewels. I worked away furiously with my crowbar hoping to be able to shout to the gang, "Look what I found." The foreman had told us, "Finders keepers." A lot of good my hard work did me; I never found a thing. Wrecking is dangerous business, and many house wreckers have been killed. After some of those brick walls had nearly fallen

[122]

on me I decided I was not going to wait to find a hidden treasure. I cut out.

My next job was with old man Smooth, Isaac Smooth's daddy. For a long time Ike and I worked for his daddy, who lived in a part of the city called the Irish Channel. I always hated to go up to the old man's house because I was afraid I might run into some of those tough Irishmen who hung out in the saloons. Old man Smooth was a whitewasher, and we helped him whitewash a huge building near those produce houses where as kids we used to collect the "soilies." Under old man Smooth's protection we had no more to fear than rabbits in a briar patch.

Ike certainly had beautiful sisters. One of them, Eva, had a very fine rooming house, and she can tell many a story about those good old days in Storyville. She has always been Ike's favorite sister, and her husband Tom was one of the best cotch players New Orleans ever had. That is saying a good deal because cotch is a tough game. It fascinated me so much that every time I could scrape up a nickel I would sit in with the four-flushing hustlers who really knew how to gamble. I always got washed out. Those boys could read my face like a book, and whenever I caught a good hand I always gave it away with a smile. Just the same the game gassed me.

chapter 8

EARLY IN 1918 the flu began to let up, and the United States started to get after the Kaiser and his boys in fine fashion. The last draft call was for men between eighteen and forty-five, so I went down to the draft board and registered. When I could feel that draft card in my hip pocket I sure was a proud fellow, expecting to go to war any minute and fight for Uncle Sam — or blow for him.

One night during that period I was waiting for something to happen and I dropped into Henry Matranga's place for a bottle of beer. The tonk was not running, but the saloon was open and some of the old-timers were standing around the bar running their mouths. I had just said hello to Matranga when Captain Jackson, the meanest guy on the police force, walked in.

"Everybody line up," he said. "We are looking for some stick-up guys who just held up a man on Rampart Street."

We tried to explain that we were innocent, but he told his men to lock us all up and take us to the Parish Prison only a block away. There I was trapped, and I had to send a message to Mayann: "Going to jail. Try to find somebody to get me out."

They did not book us right away and held us for investigation in the prison yard with the long-term prisoners waiting to go up the river. Among them were men with sentences of from forty to fifty years, guys like Dirty Dog, Steel Arm Johnny, Budow Albert Mitchel and Channey. Most of them were Creoles from the Seventh Ward where my clarinet man Barney Bigard came from.

I knew those guys when they used to come up to the Third Ward where we lived, and I remember how Black Benny told them not to start any rough stuff or they would get cleaned out. They took the warning all right. They knew Black Benny meant it. Oh, that Benny!

Among all those bad men in the prison yard I knew that there was not one who could help me. Sore Dick, the captain of the yard, was tougher than any of them. He was a short, jet-black guy, built like a brick house, who had a way of looking the newcomer over that let him know Sore Dick was boss and that he was going to run the yard the way he wanted to. I found that out soon enough. The first day we were in the yard I went up to shake hands with one of the prisoners I had known out on the street. All of a sudden somebody jabbed me in the back with a broom handle and tripped me up. When I looked up I saw Sore Dick staring at me without saying a word. It dawned on me at once that I had better get busy with the broom he was holding. All newcomers, I later found out, had to sweep out the yard whether it needed it or not. That is the way they get you in the groove before you start serving a term.

While I was in the prison yard I did not realize that Matranga had contacted his lawyer to have us all let out on parole. I did not even have to appear in court. It was part of a system that was always worked in those days. Whenever a crowd of fellows were rounded up in a raid on a gambling house or saloon the proprietor knew how to "spring" them, that is, get them out of jail.

Nevertheless, I'll never forget that experience as a stay-a-whiler with those long termers.

It's a funny thing how life can be such a drag one minute and a solid sender the next. The day I got out of jail Mardi Gras was being celebrated. It is a great day for all New Orleans, and particularly for the Zulu

Aid Pleasure and Social Club. Every member of the Club masquerades in a costume burlesquing some famous person. The King of the Zulus, also in masquerade costume, rides with six other Zulus on a float giving away coconuts as souvenirs. The members march to the good jumping music of the brass bands while the King on his throne scrapes and bows to the cheering crowds. Every year Mr. Jamke, the gravel and sand dealer, invites the King and his cortege and all the Zulus to come to his offices for champagne. He has been doing this as long as anyone can remember, and many of the Zulu members have been working for him ever since I was born.

When I ran into this celebration and the good music I forgot all about Sore Dick and the Parish Prison. Most of the members of the Zulu Club then lived around Liberty and Perdido Streets, but now Mardi Gras has become so famous — people come from all over America to see its parade — that it includes doctors, lawyers and other important people from all over the city. Later on a Lady Zulu Club was organized. It had been my life-long dream to be the King of the Zulus, as it was the dream of every kid in my neighborhood. A new king for the year is elected the day after Mardi Gras.

Garfield Carter — or Papa Gar as we called him — was the proudest stepper in the whole parade, and he had the nerve to parody Captain Jackson. He paraded disguised as the captain of the Zulu Police Force.

The crowd used to go wild when Papa Gar strutted by with his face blackened and with big white lips.

Monk Story was King of the Zulus that year, and he was a colorful character too. He could always keep a crowd doubled up with laughter at his stories, and he talked very much like Mortimer Snerd. However, he was not as good-looking. Monk was really in there that year as King of the Zulus. I finally got my wish to be King of the Zulus, and I can hardly wait for a chance to be it again.

Johnny Keeling, one of the nicest boys in our neighborhood, got into trouble with the downtown bad boys that Mardi Gras, and as usual Black Benny came to the rescue and sapped up those guys beautifully. It was better not to try to mess up the boys of our neighborhood when Black Benny was around. Of course, Black Benny had to go to jail for the job he did. But that did not make much difference. As usual he was allowed to leave the jail when he got a job to play the bass drum. As a matter of fact, the very next day Bunk Johnson went down to the prison and asked the warden to loan him Benny for Frankie Dusen's Eagle Band which was playing at a funeral. After the shindig was over Benny returned to jail with a little extra change in his pocket. Sore Dick did not throw any brooms under Black Benny's legs; if he did they would have had to build a new jail.

One time Benny had a run of luck when he was gambling at Savocas' with George Bo'hog, Red Cornelius, Black Mannie Hubbard, Sun Murray, Ben Harding and Aaron Harris. George Bo'hog was running the cotch game, and he was sore as hell at Benny because he was winning all the money. But he wasn't saying anything to Benny.

Isaiah Hubbard, Mannie's brother, was leaning on the rail around the table watching the game. He hadn't cared much for Benny for years and he insulted him every chance he had. Benny, who always tried to avoid trouble whenever possible, ignored Isaiah as much as he could, particularly since Isaiah was a tough man with his dukes. He was the only guy Benny allowed to get in his hair with slurring remarks about his ragged clothes. Isaiah himself had practically everything: money, clothes and the women who made the most money.

Isaiah was a real black man, with a thick mustache, who carried a big pistol even the cops knew he had. That day it seemed as though something had to happen. When Benny finished playing cotch he went to cash in his chips. The joint was as quiet as a church mouse when Isaiah spoke.

"You black bastard," he said to Benny. "You've won all the money, so now you can get your clothes out of hock. Now you can quit flagging that ragged ass of yours around the block."

Benny stopped in his tracks and walked right up to Isaiah.

"I don't like that remark," Benny said. "And furthermore I am tired of you slurring me. If you've got anything against me get it off your chest right now. We can settle the whole thing right here."

"No. I don't like you," Isaiah said, "and I never did."

As he said that Isaiah made a pass at Benny. Now Benny was fast on his feet; he knew something about ring fighting and he had been in a great many battle royals. He ducked and came up with a right that floored Isaiah. When this happened the crowd started to edge toward the door getting ready to cut out any minute. But they stayed when they saw it was going to be a fair fist fight, which was to Benny's advantage. They fought like two trained champions, and nobody dared to touch them. Finally Benny feinted and hit Isaiah with everything he had, which was plenty. Isaiah landed on his tail and went out like a light. Nobody said a word as Benny put his money in his pocket with tears streaming down his cheeks.

"Thank God," he said, "that's over. This man has been hounding me for years. I knew this was going to happen someday, but I never knew when. But when it did happen I knew it was going to be he or I." And he walked out.

No one said a word and no one followed Black Benny as he walked down Perdido Street shouting at the top of his voice: "Thank God, I finally got a chance to settle with Isaiah Hubbard."

As a matter of fact, Benny and Isaiah met frequently after that, but they never fought again.

Poor Benny was always getting into trouble. Now that he had won enough money he went to get his clothes out of the pawnshop where they had been for nearly a year: a nice looking brown box-back suit with thin white stripes, tan shoes from Edwin Clapps, a brown Stetson hat and a real light pink shirt with a beautiful tie. Oh, he looked very good! And we all rejoiced to see him so well dressed again. It had been raining heavily and the streets were muddy, and water from the overflowing sewers was backing up in the gutters and smelling like hell.

In those days when kegs of beer were finished they were rolled out on the sidewalk so that they could be picked up by the brewers' wagons. The fellows who hung around the neighborhood used to sit on these barrels and chew the rag. After he had gotten his clothes out of pawn Benny was sitting with the gang on a barrel — he was so happy — when a cop came up to him and told him to come to the station for questioning by the Chief of Police. The cop they had sent to bring Benny in was one of the oldest men on the force. He interrupted Benny in the midst of one of his funny stories.

"Benny," the old cop said, "the Chief of Police wants you down at the station."

"Man," Benny answered, "I haven't had these clothes on for damn near a year. There ain't no use of you or nobody trying to take me to jail, because I ain't going to jail today for nobody. Nobody. Do you get it?"

The cop insisted.

"Man, I told you," Benny repeated, "I ain't going to jail today for nobody, *no — body!* Understand?"

Just then the old policeman made a fast grab at Benny's trousers and got a good hold on them. "You're under arrest," he shouted.

Benny leapt up from the barrel like a shot and started running directly across the street with the cop still holding onto him. Benny ran so fast the cop couldn't keep up with him. The policeman slipped, lost his balance and took a header into the mud. Benny stood on the other side of the street and watched the cop pick himself up. His face was so spattered with mud that he looked like a black face comedian.

"I told you I wasn't going to jail today," Benny shouted at him, and went on about his business.

A week later Benny gave himself up. He told the Chief what had happened and what he had said to the cop. The Chief laughed and thought it was cute.

Black Benny gave me the first pistol I ever had in my life. During the Christmas and New Year's holiday season, when everybody was celebrating with pistols and firecrackers, he and some of his friends used to make the rounds of the neighborhood. Whenever they saw some kid firing a gun in the street Benny went up behind him and stuck a pistol in his back.

"I'll take this one, buddy."

The kids always forked over. I have seen Benny

come around with a basket full of guns of all kinds which he would sell for any price that was offered. Oh, what a character!

In 1918 things commenced to break for me. For a time I took Sweet Child's job hopping bells at the saloon on my corner in the Third Ward. I liked being a bell boy. All I had to do was to walk up and down the streets waiting for one of those hustling gals to stick her head out of the window and call to me.

"Bell boy," she would shout.

"Yeah," I would answer.

"Bring me half a can."

A half can meant a nickel's worth of beer. A whole can meant a dime's worth. When you bought a whole can in those days you were really celebrating. Even for a nickel they gave so much that most of the time you would have to call one of your neighbors to help you drink it up.

I kind of liked hopping bells because it gave me a chance to go into the houses and see what was going on. Lots of times when one of the gals did not have the price of a half can I would buy it for her out of the tips I had made. They were always nice to me. However, it was just my luck to have Sweet Child come back to his job. He never did lay off again.

After that I had to go back to my job on the coal wagon. As usual stepdaddy Gabe was glad to see me again, and of course I was glad to see him. Many times I tried to get Mayann to take Gabe back, but there was nothing doing. She just didn't like Gabe. I thought he was the best stepfather I ever had and I still do. Any time I wanted it I could always get a quarter out of him. Those other stepfathers of mine seemed like a bunch of cheap skates. But I just could not run Mayann's life for her.

While I was working at the coal yard Sidney Bechet, a youngster from the Creole quarter, came uptown to play at Kid Brown's, the famous parachute jumper who ran a honky-tonk at Gravier and Franklin. The first time I heard Sidney Bechet play that clarinet he stood me on my ear. I realized very soon what a versatile player he was. Every musician in town was playing in one of the bands marching in the big Labor Day parade. Somehow, though, Bechet was not working. Henry Allen, Red Allen's daddy, had come over from Algiers with his band to play for one of the lodges. Old man Allen was short a cornet, and when the bands were gathering in front of the Odd Fellow's Hall Allen spied Bechet. Allen must have known Bechet could play a lot of cornet, for he sent him into Jake Fink's to borrow a cornet from Bob Lyons, the famous bass player. Bechet joined the band and he made the whole parade, blowing like crazy. I marvelled at the way Bechet played the cornet, and I followed him all that day. There was not a cornet player in New Orleans who was like him. What feeling! What soul! Every other player in the city had to give it to him.

My next great thrill was when I played with Bechet

to advertise a prize fight. I have forgotten who was fighting, but I will never forget that I played with the great Bechet. There were only three musicians in our little band: clarinet, cornet and drums. Before I knew it, Bechet had gone up North. Then he went to Paris where he was a big hit, and still is.

chapter 9

ALONG ABOUT THE middle of the summer of 1918 Joe Oliver got an offer from Chicago to go there to play for Mrs. Major, who owned the Lincoln Gardens. He took Jimmie Noone with him to play the clarinet.

I was back on my job driving a coal cart, but I took time off to go to the train with them. Kid Ory was at the station, and so were the rest of the Ory-Oliver jazz band. It was a rather sad parting. They really didn't want to leave New Orleans, and I felt the old gang was breaking up. But in show business you always keep thinking something better's coming along.

The minute the train started to pull out I was on

my way out of the Illinois Central Station to my cart —
I had a big load of coal to deliver — when Kid Ory called
to me.

"You still blowin' that cornet?" he hollered.

I ran back. He said he'd heard a lot of talk about
Little Louis. (That's what most folks called me when I
was in my teens, I was so little and so cute.)

"Hmmm . . ." I pricked up my ears.

He said that when the boys in the band found out
for sure that Joe Oliver was leaving, they told him to go
get Little Louis to take Joe's place. He was a little in
doubt at first, but after he'd looked around the town he
decided I was the right one to have a try at taking that
great man's place. So he told me to go wash up and
then come play a gig with them that very same night.

What a thrill that was! To think I was considered
up to taking Joe Oliver's place in the best band in town!
I couldn't hardly wait to get to Mayann's to tell her the
good news. I'd been having so many bad breaks, I just
had to make a beeline to Mayann's.

Mayann was the one who'd always encouraged me
to carry on with my cornet blowing because I loved it
so much.

I couldn't phone her because we didn't have
phones in our homes in those days — only the filthy rich
could afford phones, and we were far from being in that
class.

I wasn't particular about telling Mama Lucy
just yet about my success, because she would always give

me a dirty dig of some kind. Like the night I played my first job. That was more of a hustle than anything else; in fact, I didn't make but fifteen cents. I sure was proud to bring that money home to my mother. Mama Lucy heard me tell my mother:

"Mama, here's what we made last night. Saturday night, too. We worked for tips, and fifteen cents was all we made, each of us."

My sister raised up out of a sound sleep and said: "Hmmm! Blow your brains out for fifteen cents!"

I wanted to kill her. Mama had to separate us to keep us from fighting that morning.

So when I got my first big break from Kid Ory, I looked up my mother first, instead of my sister. I just let Lucy find it out for herself. And then when Lucy praised me with enthusiasm, I just casually said:

"Thanks, sis."

Cute, huh? But inwardly I was glad they were happy for me. The first night I played with Kid Ory's band, the boys were so surprised they could hardly play their instruments for listening to me blow up a storm. But I wasn't frightened one bit. I was doing everything just exactly the way I'd heard Joe Oliver do it. At least I tried to. I even put a big towel around my neck when the band played a ball down at Economy Hall. That was the first thing Joe always did — he'd put a bath towel around his neck and open up his collar underneath so's he could blow free and easy.

And because I'd listened to Joe all the time he was

with Kid Ory I knew almost everything that band played, by ear anyway. I was pretty fast on my horn at that time, and I had a good ear. I could catch on real fast.

Kid Ory was so nice and kind, and he had so much patience, that first night with them was a pleasure instead of a drag. There just wasn't a thing for me to do except blow my head off. Mellow moments, I assure you.

After that first gig with the Kid I was in. I began to get real popular with the dance fans as well as the musicians. All the musicians came to hear us and they'd hire me to play in their bands on the nights I wasn't engaged by Kid Ory.

I was doing great, till the night I got the biggest scare of my life. I was taking the cornet player's place in the Silver Leaf Band, a very good band too. All the musicians in that band read the music of their parts. The clarinet player was Sam Dutrey, the brother of Honore Dutrey, the trombonist. Sam was one of the best clarinetists in town. (He also cut hair on the side.) He had an airy way about him that'd make one think he was stuck up, but he was really just a jolly, good-natured fellow and liked to joke a lot. But I didn't know that!

The night I was to fill in for the clarinet player, I went early to sort of compose myself, because since I was playing with a strange band I didn't want anything to go wrong if I could help it. Most of the band began straggling in one by one about fifteen minutes before hitting time. Sam Dutrey was the last to arrive. I had never seen him before in my life. So while we were warming up and getting in tune, Sam came up on the bandstand. He said good evening to the fellows in the band and then he looked directly at me.

"What the hell is this?" he roared. "Get offa here, boy!" He had a real voice.

I was real scared. "Yassuh," I said. I started to pack up my cornet.

Then one of the men said: "Leave the boy alone, Sam. He's working in Willie's place tonight." Then he introduced me to Sam.

Sam laughed and said: "I was only kidding, son."

"Yassuh," I still said.

The whole night went down with us, swinging up a mess. But still I had that funny feeling. Sometimes now I run into Sam Dutrey, and we almost laugh ourselves sick over that incident.

Sam and Honore both were tops on their instruments. Honore Dutrey had one of the finest tones there could be had out of a trombone. But he messed up his life while he was in the Navy. One day aboard ship he fell asleep in a powder magazine and gassed himself so badly he suffered from asthma for years afterward. It always bothered him something terrible blowing his trombone.

When I had the band in Chicago in 1926, playing for Joe Glaser, who's now my personal manager, Dutrey was the trombone player. He would do real fine on all the tunes except the *Irish Medley,* in which the brass had to stay in the upper register at the ending. That's when Dutrey would have to go behind the curtains and gush his atomizer into his nostrils. Then he would say, "Take 'em on down." Well, you never heard such fine strong trombone in all your life. I'll come back to Honore later.

There's lots of musicians I'll be mentioning, especially the ones I played with and had dealings with from time to time. All in all, I had a wonderful life playing with them. Lots of them were characters, and when I say "characters" I mean *characters!* I've played with some of the finest musicians in the world, jazz and classic. God bless them, all of them!

While I was playing just gigs with Kid Ory's band we all had jobs during the day. The war was still going full blast and the orders were: "Work or Fight." And since I was too young to fight, I kept on driving my coal cart. Outside the cornet, it seemed like the coal cart was the only job I enjoyed working. Maybe it was because of all those fine old-timers.

Kid Ory had some of the finest gigs, especially for the rich white folks. Whenever we'd play a swell place, such as the Country Club, we would get more money, and during the intermissions the people giving the dance would see that the band had a big delicious meal, the same as they ate. And by and by the drummer and

I would get in with the colored waiters and have enough food to take home to Mayann and Mama Lucy.

The music-reading musicians like those in Robechaux's band thought that we in Kid Ory's band were good, but only good together. One day those big shots had a funeral to play, but most of them were working during the day and couldn't make it. So they engaged most of Ory's boys, including me. The day of the funeral the musicians were congregating at the hall where the Lodge started their march, to go up to the dead brother's house. Kid Ory and I noticed all those stuck-up guys giving us lots of ice. They didn't feel we were good enough to play their marches.

I nudged Ory, as if to say, "You dig what I'm diggin'?"

Ory gave me a nod, as if to say yes, he digged.

We went up to the house playing a medium fast march. All the music they gave us we played, and a lot easier than they did. They still didn't say anything to us one way or the other.

Then they brought the body out of the house and we went on to the cemetery. We were playing those real slow funeral marches. After we reached the cemetery, and they lowered the body down six feet in the ground, and the drummer man rolled on the drums, they struck a ragtime march which required swinging from the band. And those old fossils just couldn't cut it. That's when we Ory boys took over and came in with flying colors.

We were having that good old experience, swinging that whole band! It sounded so good!

The second line — the raggedy guys who follow parades and funerals to hear the music — they enjoyed what we played so much they made us take an encore. And that don't happen so much in street parades.

We went into the hall swinging the last number, *Panama*. I remembered how Joe Oliver used to swing that last chorus in the upper register, and I went on up there and got those notes, and the crowd went wild.

After that incident those stuck-up guys wouldn't let us alone. They patted us on the back and just wouldn't let us alone. They hired us several times afterward. After all, we'd proved to them that any learned musician can read music, but they can't all swing. It was a good lesson for them.

Several times later they asked us to join their band, but I had already given Celestin (another fine cornet player, and the leader of the Tuxedo Brass Band) my consent to join him and replace Sidney Desvigne, another real good and fancy cornet man. Personally I thought Celestin's Tuxedo Band was the hottest in town since the days of the Onward Brass Band with Emmanuel Perez and Joe Oliver holding down the cornet section. My, my, what a band! So after Joe Oliver went to Chicago, the Tuxedo Brass Band got all the funerals and parades.

More about Papa Celestin later.

The last time I saw Lady, the mule I used to drive,

was November 11, 1918, the day the Armistice was signed, the day the United States and the rest of the Allies cut the German Kaiser and his army a brand 'noo one. At eleven o'clock that morning I was unloading coal at Fabacher's restaurant on St. Charles Street, one of the finest restaurants in town. I was carrying the coal inside and sweating like mad when I heard several automobiles going down St. Charles Street with great big tin cans tied to them, dragging on the ground and making all kinds of noise. After quite a few cars had passed I got kind of curious and asked somebody standing nearby, "What's all the fuss about?"

"They're celebratin' 'cause the war is over," he said to me.

When he said that, it seemed as though a bolt of lightning struck me all over.

I must have put about three more shovels of coal into the wheelbarrow to take inside, when all of a sudden a thought came to me. "The war is over. And here I am monkeyin' around with this mule. Huh!"

I immediately dropped that shovel, slowly put on my jacket, looked at Lady and said: "So long, my dear. I don't think I'll ever see you again." And I cut out, leaving mule cart, load of coal and everything connected with it. I haven't seen them since.

I ran straight home. Mayann, noticing I was home much earlier than usual, asked me what was the matter, trouble?

"No, mother," I said. "The war is over, and I quit

the coal yard job for the last time. Now I can play my music the way I want to. And when I want to."

The very next day all the lights went on again. And all the places commenced opening up in droves. Oh, the city sure did look good again, with all those beautiful lights along Canal Street, and all the rest. Matranga called me to come back to play in his honky-tonk, but he was too late. I was looking forward to bigger things, especially since Kid Ory had given me the chance to play the music I really wanted to play. And that was all kinds of music, from jazz to waltzes.

Then Kid Ory really did get a log of gigs. He even started giving his own dances, Monday nights downtown at the Economy Hall. Monday night was a slow night in New Orleans at that time, and we didn't get much work other places. But Kid Ory did so well at the Economy Hall that he kept it up for months and made a lot of dough for himself. He paid us well too.

A lot of Saturday nights we didn't work either, so on those nights I would play over in Gretna, across the river, at the Brick House, another honky-tonk. This was a little town near Algiers, Red Allen's home, which paid pretty well, including the tips from the drunken customers, the whores, the pimps and the gamblers.

There also were some real bad characters who hung around the joint, and you could get your head cut off, or blown off, if you weren't careful.

We had a three-piece band, and we had to play a

lot of blues to satisfy those hustling women who made quite a bit of money selling themselves very cheap.

The Brick House was located right by the levee and the Jackson Avenue ferry. Going back home to New Orleans on the Jackson Avenue streetcar after we finished work at the Brick House used to frighten me a lot because there weren't many people out that time of the morning. Just a few drunks, white and colored. Lots of times the two races looked as if they were going to get into a scrap over just nothing at all. And down there, with something like that happening and only a few Spades (colored folks) around, it wasn't so good. Even if we colored ones were right, when the cops arrived they'd whip our heads first and ask questions later.

One night when just a few colored people, including me, were coming back from Gretna in the wee hours of the morning, a middle-aged colored woman was sitting on a bench by the railing of the boat, lushed to the gills. The deckhands were washing the floor and it was very slippery. Just before the boat pulled off an elderly white lady came running up the gangplank and just managed to make the ferry. Not knowing the floor was wet, she slipped and almost fell. Immediately the colored woman raised up and looked at the white one and said: "Thank God!"

Talk about your tense moments!

My, my, the Lord was with us colored people that night, because nothing happened. I'm still wondering why. I have seen trouble start down there from less than that.

Louis Armstrong met his first wife at the Brick House. But before I tell you how I got to know Daisy Parker, I want to take one last look again at the good old days of Storyville.

For instance, I haven't said anything yet about Lulu White. Poor Lulu White! What a woman!

I admired her even when I was a kid, not because of the great business she was in, but because of the great business she made of her Mahogany Hall. That was the name of the house she ran at Storyville. It was a pleasure house, where those rich ofay (white) business men and planters would come from all over the South and spend some awful large amounts of loot.

Lulu had some of the biggest diamonds anyone would want to look at. Some of the finest furs. . . . And some of the finest yellow gals working for her. . . .

Champagne would flow like water at Lulu's. If anyone walked in and ordered a bottle of beer, why, they'd look at him twice and then — maybe — they'd serve it. And if they did, you'd be plenty sorry you didn't order champagne.

Jelly Roll Morton made a lot of money playing the piano for Lulu White, playing in one of her rooms.

Of course when the drop came and the Navy and the law started clamping down on Storyville, Lulu had to close down too. She had enough salted away to retire for life and forget all about the business. But no, she was like a lot of sporting house landladies I've known through life — they were never satisfied and would not let well enough alone, and would try to make that big fast money regardless of the law showering down on them.

Mayor Martin Behrman made them cut out from Storyville within days. Lulu White moved from 325 North Basin Street to 1200 Bienville Street, and tried her luck at another house. That's where she did the wrong thing, to try to continue running her house with the law on her like white on rice, taking all the loot she'd made over the years along with her diamonds and jewelry and all.

I remember Detective Harry Gregson gave her a real tough time. He was a tough man, and he's still living. All the dicks in Storyville — Hessel, Fast Mail, Gregson, the others — I got to know when as a kid I delivered hard coal to all of those cribs where the girls used to stand in their doorways and work as the men went by.

There were all kinds of thrills for me in Storyville. On every corner I could hear music. And such good music! The music I wanted to hear. It was worth my salary — the little I did get — just to go into Storyville. It seemed as though all the bands were shooting at each other with those hot riffs. And that man Joe Oliver! My, my, that man kept me spellbound with that horn of his. . . .

Storyville! With all those glorious trumpets — Joe

Oliver, Bunk Johnson — he was in his prime then — Emmanuel Perez, Buddy Petit, Joe Johnson — who was real great, and it's too bad he didn't make some records. . . .

It struck me that Joe Johnson and Buddy Petit had the same identical styles. Which was great! In fact all the trumpet and cornet players who were playing in my young days in New Orleans were hellions — that's the biggest word I can say for them. They could play those horns for hours on end.

But Joe Oliver, a fat man, was the strongest and the most creative. And Bunk Johnson was the sweetest. Bunk cut everybody for tone, though they all had good tones. That was the first thing Mr. Peter Davis taught me—out in the Colored Waifs' Home for Boys. "Tone," he said. "A musician with a tone can play any kind of music, whether it's classical or ragtime."

It seemed like everyone was pulling for Lulu White to give up and lead a decent life. But she just wouldn't. She held on to her horses and her carriage and her Negro driver as long as she could. But the law she defied dragged her down like a dog until they broke her completely. It was a shame the way they snatched her mansion — furniture, diamonds galore, things worth a fortune.

Oh well, although Lulu's gone, the name of Mahogany Hall on Basin Street will live forever. And so will Basin Street.

chapter 10

THE BRICK HOUSE, in Gretna, Louisiana . . .

In all my whole career the Brick House was one of the toughest joints I ever played in. It was the honky-tonk where levee workers would congregate every Saturday night and trade with the gals who'd stroll up and down the floor and into the bar. Those guys would drink and fight one another like circle saws. Bottles would come flying over the bandstand like crazy, and there was lots of just plain common shooting and cutting. But somehow all of that jive didn't faze me at all, I was so happy to have some place to blow my horn.

For about three Saturday nights straight I kept

noticing one of the gals looking at me with the stuff in her eyes. I kept on playing, but I started giving her that righteous look in return. That chick was Daisy Parker.

Of course, it was strictly business with her. And to me it was just another mash — that's what we called flirting in those days. We would use the expression, "The lady has a mash on you," and then we would poke our chests 'way out as if we were pretty important.

Anyhow I did not find that out on my first meeting with Daisy, until I was in one of the rooms upstairs in the Brick House. She stated her price, which wasn't much in those days, so I told her I would see her after I finished work. She agreed and away I went, thinking: "Hmmm, but that's a good-looking Creole gal." I didn't know what I was in for.

Sure enough, after work I made a beeline upstairs, and Daisy excused herself from her party and met me there. Since she was through work and I was too, we stayed in that room from five in the morning till 'way into the afternoon.

The first thing I noticed about Daisy that night — but I didn't say anything because I didn't want to believe my eyes — was that when she undressed she pulled off a pair of "sides," artificial hips she wore to give herself a good figure. I thought to myself: "Hmm, as much as I've been admiring this chick and her shape, here she comes bringing me a pair of waterwings." But before I could think another thing, she came out with the explanation. She said she was too skinny and only weighed less than a hundred pounds. The way she was built caused her to wear them. And they did give her a pretty fair shape. She was right, too, because along with her good looks, she was still "reet" with me. So I got used to it; in fact I even got used to seeing her put them on, and loved it.

We had several meetings after that, and Daisy and I commenced to fall deeply in love with each other.

Daisy was twenty-one years of age, and I was eighteen. I was so gone over her we never mentioned that she had an "Old Man" — the name we used to have for a common law husband — though that was the first thing I usually asked a chick. Later on I found the reason for Daisy not telling me about the drummer who played in another honky-tonk in Gretna while she worked in the Brick House; the customers who visited the Brick House paid more money.

She and this drummer lived in Freetown, a little village between Gretna and Algiers. Since she kept on asking me to come over to her house and visit her some afternoon, I had just taken it for granted that she was living by herself, the same as a lot of other working girls I had played around with. Their pimps would come around and collect, do what comes naturally, and cut out either to their bachelor's quarters or home to their wives and kids.

Since Kid Ory had signed a contract to play at the rich folks' New Orleans Country Club every Saturday night, I put the Brick House down quicker'n I'd left Lady on Armistice Day. So for a whole month I didn't see Daisy, just talked to her on the telephone every now and then. She didn't know how to get over to the New Orleans side of the river because she'd spent all her life in Gretna and other little towns in Louisiana.

I wanted to see Daisy so bad — as bad as she wanted to see me — that I decided one afternoon to put on my sharpest vine. I didn't have but one, and I treasured it by keeping it cleaned and pressed all the time. It was about two in the afternoon when I was ready to leave. Mayann, with whom I was still living at that time, asked me: "Where are you goin', son? Looking so good and dressed up . . ."

I said: "Aw, nowheres in particular, mama. Just feel like putting on my Sunday-go-to-meeting suit."

She gave a good hearty chuckle and went into the kitchen to stir that fine pot of red beans and rice, which sure did smell good. I almost changed my mind when I got a whiff of them.

It must have been around three-thirty when I reached Freetown. The bus I'd taken from Gretna stopped about three-quarters of a mile from where Daisy lived. I asked someone how to get to her house, which was easy to find as it was in the country, and everyone knows everyone else in the country.

It was a four-room house, with the rooms one behind the other. You could stand at the front door and look all the way back to the kitchen. It was an old house, with poorly lighted rooms and a beat-up porch.

The minute I knocked at the door, Daisy appeared, all smiles. She led me into the parlor, and the minute she closed the door we kissed — a long one. Then she took my hat and laid it on the old-fashioned sewing machine she had. Then she sat on my lap and we were really swinging with the kisses when, all of a sudden, a rap came on the door.

"Who is it?" Daisy said, all excited.

That knocker happened to be her old man, who, to my surprise, had been hearing about me and Daisy canoeing from the first night we'd got together. He pushed in the door real hard and came in. Daisy jumped off my knee and ran into the next room, with him right behind her.

For a moment I thought of a million things. The first was the incident with Irene and Cheeky Black.

Just then I heard something hit the floor. Yep, it was Daisy. He had hit her a hard blow, and without saying a word, without even hollering, she went out like a light.

I commenced getting real busy getting out of there. As plainly as Daisy had put my hat on the sewing machine, and as easy as it was to get to, I just couldn't seem to find it and put it on my head fast enough. All the time I kept imagining what was coming for me next.

I finally did get out before he came in from the back room, but the whole time I was making it for that bus I never did get my hat on. In fact, I didn't even think of putting it on my head until I was safely on the ferry boat going back to New Orleans. I was, you see, still a kid when I found out it was better to run with your hat in your hand instead of on your head — you make better time.

When I hit that ferry boat I let out a big sigh. And I said to myself: "Ump! Once again, never again."

Then I thought of how I'd said the same words when Cheeky Black caught Irene and me in the room together. But this time I meant it.

When I got back home to Mayann I was all upset. But I did a pretty fair job in not letting her see any signs of trouble on my face. She worried a great deal about Mama Lucy and me, because we used to get into trouble on the spur of the moment. She fixed supper — beans and rice — and the minute I put the first mouthful into my chops I forgot all about the mess.

I didn't see Daisy for almost a month after that scrimmage. I decided to give her up as a bad job anyway. Then, too, Mayann didn't know about her. For one reason or another I just wouldn't tell about Daisy. And since I had decided to give her up, there just wasn't anything to tell.

Time went by, and then one day who should come around my neighborhood of Liberty and Perdido Streets looking for me, but Daisy! I was really surprised. Because the way she lied to me about her old man, I didn't think she really cared for me. I thought right away she was only using me for a playtoy or some thing.

I was speechless when she saw me standing on the corner with all the old-timers who'd just come from work in the coal yards, and ran up to me and kissed me with tears in her eyes, saying: "Darling, I've been so lonesome, blue, and unhappy, I just couldn't stand it any longer. I just had to see you."

All the guys were watching me and saying: "Go on, Dipper! You with a fine looking gal like that pouring out her heart to you! Man, you must have really laid it."

Then it dawned on me that it was kind of nice to be able to signify in front of them for a change, with a fine chick breaking down all over me.

Then I caught a-hold of myself and asked her: "Er—what—how did you get over on this side, honey?"

Then she told me her cousin showed her the way as he went to work at his job on Canal Street.

We went to Rampart and Lafayette Streets, to Kid Green's Hotel, and engaged a room for the evening so we could talk over many things.

Kid Green was an ex-prizefighter and was known from one end of the United States to the other. He was a good one in his day, but now he had retired on the money he'd saved. He had a pretty fair hotel, not the best in the world, but comfortable. He and I were good friends, and whenever I'd go there with a chick, he'd make room for me no matter how crowded he was. Kid Green had a reputation for wearing those "Stock

Ties" which were very popular in those days; they are made of shirt goods, or silk, and are wrapped around the neck and tied with a great big knot in front. He was a master at wearing them. Every tooth in his head was gold, and there was a big diamond inserted in one of the front ones, the same as Jelly Roll Morton had. Kid Green had so much gold in his mouth they called him "Klondike," and when he smiled, you could see gold for miles and miles.

While I was with Daisy at Kid Green's Hotel I had a good chance to really check up on her. I wouldn't say that she was "beautiful but dumb," because she was pretty clever and really knew how to make money. But she was very jealous.

I figured out that during Daisy's childhood in the country she had evidently been spoiled by her parents who let her have her own way and do whatever she pleased. She would play hookey from school whenever she wanted, and she grew up without any vocation or learning at all, not even a middle grade learning, which any ordinary kid would get in life. Later I found out she couldn't even read or write. All she knew how to do was fuss and fight.

But it's a funny thing about two people being in love — whatever little traits there are, no matter how unpleasant they may be, love will drown them out. So since I realized I was in love with Daisy for sure, I did not fight with myself any longer, and I gave over to my lovely feeling for her. Because she really did move me greatly. And that was that. . . .

When we left Kid Green's Hotel we went straight down to City Hall and got hitched. And that was when the lid blew off.

Before we got out of the City Hall, the news had spread all over my neighborhood. The old-timers such as Mrs. Magg, Mrs. Laura, Mrs. Martin, were surprised, of course, but they were the ones who were actually glad for me. But the rest of the neighborhood, especially those old gossipers, made a beeline for Mayann.

They all upset Mayann by asking her: "Are you going to let him marry that whore?"

And Mayann (bless her heart!) told them very calmly: "Well, that's my son, and he has to live his own life." She shrugged her shoulders. "And he loves the woman enough to marry her, that's his business, and they both have my blessing. And I will also try my best to make her as happy as I can."

So the crowd, after seeing her point, agreed with her as they walked away.

After Daisy and I came out of the City Hall she caught a streetcar and went back to Freetown to pack up her clothes. I went home.

On my way I ran into Black Benny, standing on the corner in his soldier's uniform. Although the war had ended, he was still in the Army, waiting to be discharged. He was a sergeant and could give orders still to the guys who were under him. At this time he had run into another soldier who had a lower ranking than he, and the guy in civilian life was one of those snobbish kind of fellows who gave Black Benny a tough time through life. So this day Benny waited until the private almost passed him, and then Benny hollered: "ATTENTION!!!" So the guy stood at attention, while Benny went all around the block, leaving the guy with his hand up, saluting. Finally Benny came back and said, "At ease!," and the guy went away with an awful frown. But he dared not say anything to Black Benny about it. Because Benny was a man among men, you can take it from me.

When I came home, Mayann and I had a real heart-to-heart talk. First thing she asked me was: "Son, are you sure you love this girl?"

I said: "Mother, I've never been surer of anything in my whole life as my love for Daisy. She has convinced me that she's the woman for me."

Well," mother said, "I hear she hasn't got much learning."

"Mother," I said, "what's that got to do with our being in love with each other? You must realize that I didn't go any further than fifth grade in school myself. But with my good sense and mother-wit, and knowing how to treat and respect the feelings of other people, that's all I've needed through life. You taught me that, mother. And I haven't done so bad at it. Ain't that right?"

Mayann shrugged her shoulders. "I guess you're right, son." Then she said: "You must bring your wife to me; I want to meet her."

With a palpitating heart I gave a big sigh of relief and said: "Oh, thanks, mom."

Mayann was the one I wanted the o.k. from. I didn't much care about what anybody else said.

I gave my dear mother a great big hug and a kiss, and made a beeline to Daisy. I told her of the good news, and she was *so* happy that Mayann was satisfied with our marriage in spite of all the old gossipers in the neighborhood.

For a month or more Daisy and I only met a different places and hotels, because we didn't have enough money to get a place of our own. Then one day we found a two-room flat over an upholstering place on Melpomene Street in uptown New Orleans. The place we had was nothing elaborate. In order to get to where we lived we had to go by way of some stairs on the outside, the alley side. When it rained, it was something awful. The garbage that had been piled there for ages by the upholsterer-landlord and the other tenants who lived in the back yard made it very unpleasant for me to go home there from work every night. But it was a place to live, and a little place of privacy, and we could call it our own. So we gladly made the best of it.

The place we lived in had two porches, a front one, and one in the back; but we called them "galleries," as the word "porch" was unheard of to us then. We lived on the second floor, and our gallery was an old one; it had begun to slant a little, and when it rained the water would run down it like down a wall.

One day when it was raining like mad, Daisy and I were in the front room listening to some new records I had just bought, new releases of the original Dixieland Jazz Band, which we were playing on an upright Victrola we were very proud of. The records were *Livery Stable Blues* and *Tiger Rag*, the first *Tiger Rag* to be recorded. (Between you and me, it's still the best.)

Clarence, my cousin Flora Miles' illegitimate son, was living with us at the time. He was about three years old and still in dresses. Down there all kids wore dresses until they were a real large size. Kids love to wander around a house, and Clarence was no exception. On this rainy day — big sheets of rain were falling — Clarence was playing with some toys I had bought for him. He was in the rear room, which was the kitchen for us, and we didn't notice him when he wandered out of the kitchen on to the back porch, where it was raining terribly hard.

All of a sudden, when Daisy and I were playing records, we heard Clarence crying frantically. So we ran to the rear door to see what was the matter. I was real frightened when I looked on the rear porch and couldn't see him, but I could hear him crying. Then I looked down to the ground, and there was Clarence coming up the steps crying and holding his head. He had slipped off the porch, it was so wet, and fallen to the ground. The average child probably would have gotten killed, but for Clarence the fall only set him back behind the average child.

That fall hindered Clarence all through his life. I had some of the best doctors anyone could get examine him, and they all agreed that the fall had made him feeble-minded. His mind is four years behind the average child's.

I took him to all kinds of schools as he grew. I also enrolled him in a Catholic school; they kept him there several months and then sent him back to me saying the same as the rest said. I got so disgusted with all the running around they were giving Clarence I decided to take over and teach him myself.

And since Clarence has always been a nervous sort of fellow and was never able to work and earn his own living, I set up a routine for him in which he'd be happy the rest of his days. I managed to teach him the necessary things in life, such as being courteous, having respect for other people, and last but not least, having good common sense. I always managed to have someone look after Clarence whenever I had to travel or go to work. The musicians, actors — in fact, everybody whom I'd ever introduced Clarence to — they've all taken a liking to him right away. As we used to say in New Orleans, Clarence never was a "sassy child."

During those days, when I wasn't playing with Kid Ory in a funeral or a parade or an advertising stint, I would be at the head of the New Basin Canal, hanging around the charcoal schooners. We youngsters would wait for them to clean the big lumps of coal, put them in large burlap sacks, and then throw the small pieces into a corner of the schooner. We would buy small pieces from them. We would carry them away in big burlap sacks, put them in water buckets and sell them at houses for five cents a bucket. That is how I earned my living when I married Daisy.

Handling and selling charcoal was certainly a dirty job. My face and hands were always black, and most of the time I looked like Al Jolson when he used to get down on his knees and sing *Mammy*. But with that job and playing music I made a good living.

Whenever Daisy and I had a fuss — and how I hated it — I would put my clothes and Clarence's clothes into my charcoal sack and the two of us would move down to my mother's house intending to stay there forever. Then, two weeks later, along would come Daisy. She would make all kinds of apologies and promise never to upset me again and let me blow my trumpet in peace.

One day a member of my club, The Tammany Social Aid and Pleasure Club, died. The funeral left from the corner of Liberty and Perdido Streets. All the members had to wear black or real dark suits, and I had been lucky enough to get my black broadcloth suit out of pawn in time for the funeral. In those days we did a good bit of pawning. As soon as a guy got broke the first thing he thought of was the pawn shop. All out of pawn that day, I looked like a million dollars.

Living in our neighborhood was a gal named Rella Martin with whom I used to sweetheart. Somehow Daisy found out about this chick. She did not say anything about it to me but I suspected something was bugging her from the way she used to give me hell every time I came home only a half an hour late. Then we would just about tear the roof off the place calling each other nice names.

That day of the funeral, while the body was still in the church, I was standing on the corner talking to Rella and a dear friend of mine named Little Head with whom I had gone to the Fisk School. It had been raining all morning; the gutters were full of water and the streets real muddy. I had on a brand new Stetson hat (like the one in the song *St. James Infirmary*), my fine black suit and new patent leather shoes. Believe me, I was a sharp cat. The three of us were talking about nothing in particular, just killing time while we waited to walk the body to the cemetery. I was one of the pall bearers. All of a sudden I saw Daisy coming in our direction. "Oh, oh, now there will be trouble," I thought.

"Folks," I said, "there's Daisy coming down the street."

They knew what a jealous woman she was. Rella thought it best to leave me and Little Head standing there alone. As Daisy came closer we did not say a word and neither did she. Instead she whipped out her razor and began cursing. I swung around and started to run. I was fast on my feet and I made a fast start. As I jumped over the gutter my hat fell off, my good old John B. Stetson. That was *the* hat in those days, and I had struggled and saved a long time to buy it. Little Head was about to lean over and pick it up for me when Daisy rushed up to him and made a long swipe at his rear. He was off in a flash like me.

Daisy was so furious she picked up my hat and started cutting it to ribbons. My Gawd! Did that burn me up! I was about to go back and have it out with her when my club fellows grabbed me and told me I could not win.

"Look out boy! She's got a razor. You haven't even got a penknife."

By this time Daisy had cut my hat to pieces and was starting back uptown. I was foaming at the mouth, but I took the boys' advice and let her cut out. But God knows I wasn't going to forget about what she had done.

Just then the members started coming out of the church to the sad boom, boom, boom of the bass drum. Then the brass band struck up *Nearer My God to Thee* and we were on our way to the cemetery. All the time I was marching (with another boy's hat on in place of my cut-up one) I kept thinking about what Daisy had done to me in front of my friends, the members of the Tammany Social Club. The cemetery was not far from where Daisy and I lived. After the body was buried I did not wait to join the members as they marched back to the hall. I was so angry with Daisy I cut out at once and went straight home.

When I got home Daisy was not in. She was sitting at the window of her friend's house with about ten bricks sitting beside her. But I did not know this. Just as I was about to put the key in the lock one of Daisy's bricks hit our door. Wham! This really scared me. To my surprise, when I turned to see where the bricks were coming from, I saw Daisy cursing and throwing bricks faster than Satchel Paige. There was not anything I could do but keep on ducking bricks until her supply ran out. And when it did she came flying downstairs to fight it out with me. Quick as a flash I stooped down and picked up one of the bricks she had thrown at me. I cocked up my right leg as though I was going to pitch a strike for the home team and let the brick fly. It hit Daisy right in the stomach. She doubled up in a knot screaming: "You've killed me. You've killed me."

I don't know what else she said because I was not there to hear it. Someone had called the police station (people will do those things) saying a man and a woman were fighting, and they were certainly right. When I heard the patrol bell ringing I tore out for the back fence and sailed over it so fast I did not even touch it. I could hear the policemen blowing their whistles and shooting their pistols into the air to try to stop me. That did not faze me. I was gone like the turkey through the corn.

When the police are called to stop a fighting couple

and find only one of them, they take that one to prison. That is what happened to Daisy. In spite of all her hollering, screaming and cursing they hauled her off. She raised particular hell with those cops. While they were trying to put her into the partol wagon she kicked one of them under the chin. He was so angry he hit her cute little Creole head with his licorice stick, making her head bleed terribly. She did not dare report that to the captain of the police because that same cop would have laid for her when she got out of jail and given her another head whipping. That is what the New Orleans cops did in those days.

Daisy played it smart. She went to jail crying like an innocent babe regardless of all the hell she had just raised. Just like a woman.

In the meantime I had run back and caught up with my club's funeral, borrowed another good hat from a friend of mine who was a bystander and forgot all about the one Daisy had cut to ribbons. In those days when a fellow wore a John B. Stetson he was really a big shot, as big shots went at that time. We poor young musicians would have to save for months to get the fifteen dollars those hats cost then. We wanted them so badly we would save every nickel we could spare, but even at that some of the boys could not make the grade. They would pay a deposit on one of them and would nearly finish paying the instalments when they would run short of money. Then the hat store would sell the hat they had been paying for to someone else. Now you can see why I got so angry with Daisy for cutting my hat to pieces. But as I say I forgot all about it when I heard that brass band showering down on one of those real fine funeral marches. Those brass bands could play a funeral march so sweet and with so much soul you could actually feel it inside.

While I was walking in the funeral procession a fellow ran up to me and gave me a message from Daisy, who was still in jail and not even booked. It must have been one of the jail trusties because no one else could have found that out so soon. As I explained about Black Benny, a trustie can go out on the street whenever he wants to, and can make money running errands for the other prisoners. I gave the guy with the message a couple of bucks and he told me Daisy was not even booked. Mad at her as I had been, I softened up right away. I told the messenger to tell Daisy not to worry, that I still loved her and that all was forgotten.

Luckily at that time I was still working on the boats, and my boss thought an awful lot of me. I knew that if I asked him to get Daisy out of jail he would do it quicker than I could say jackrabbit. As soon as the funeral was over I gave my pal back his John B. Stetson, thanked him, and made a beeline for the nearest grocery in our neighborhood. We always had to go to the grocery store to phone or receive a message.

I always kept in the good graces of the grocery man. It is important to be able to use his phone and to have him take messages for you, but even more important is the good credit he can let you have. All my gigs used to come in by phone, and old Tony, Mr.

Louis Armstrong, shortly after he joined King Oliver's
Creole Jazz Band in Chicago, 1923.

Louis, about 1930.

The *Sydney* band plays again thirty years later: Warren "Baby" Dodds on the drums, George "Pops" Foster slapping bass, Louis Armstrong with his trumpet.

Louis Armstrong with two admirers, actor William Lang-
ford and Tallulah Bankhead (1950).

Chicago's Mayor Martin H. Kennelly officially welcomes Louis Armstrong to his city in 1951. Louis was the first musician to be given this honor.

Louis meets a young fan in Switzerland on his tour of
Europe in 1952.

Two old masters meet: Louis Armstrong and Lionel
Hampton.

Louis Armstrong and his wife Lucille.

Gaspar, Matranga, or Segretta never failed to let me know. That goes to show that no matter how tough an ofay may seem, there is always some "black son of a bitch" he is wild about and loves to death just like one of his own relatives.

The day I called up my boss on the boat he immediately phoned the police station and had Daisy paroled. Of course I went down to the police station and waited to take her home. I noticed she was limping a little in her left leg when she came out. For a moment she was glad to see me, and we kissed and made up. Then we started to walk toward the firing line where she had thrown all those bricks at me. (Thank God she was such a bad shot.)

The nearer home we got the more she began to think about our fight. I could see by the expression on her face that she was getting more and more angry. I still did not say a word about it. Anyhow she could not pretend any longer. All of a sudden she turned on me and started to curse and call me all kinds of dirty names. She said I had crippled her and that she was going to get revenge if it was the last thing she did. That struck me as a very, very strange thing for her to say to me, especially as I had begun to think that everything was all right, and that we had thrown away the hatchet for good! What is more, we were even. She had cut my hat to ribbons and swung on me and my friend. When I went home she had showered a whole flock of bricks at me as well as everything else she could get her hands on.

So when Daisy started her angry jive at me on the streetcar I said to myself: "Well, boy, you better get ready for another one of Daisy's cheap scenes." For every name she called me I called her the same, and I hit her with a few real hard ones for lagniappe (or good measure), which is what we kids called the tokens of thanks the grocer gave us when we went there to pay the bill for our parents. We would get animal crackers or almost anything that did not cost very much for lagniappe, and the grocer who gave the most lagniappe would get the most trade from us kids.

When we reached Melpomene and Dryades Streets near home we were still arguing like mad. After we got off the car we met a policeman patrolling the beat who happened to know me from my playing with Kid Ory's band in a lot of benefits around town. Instead of throwing the two of us back in jail he gave us a break.

"Dipper mouth," he said, "Why don't you take your wife home off the street before some other cop comes along and arrests the two of you."

That certainly made me feel good. I was recognized by one of the toughest policemen on the force. Instead of giving me a head whipping as the police usually did, he gave me advice and protected me.

When Daisy and I reached our little two-roomer the first thing I did was to lay my cards on the table and have a heart-to-heart talk with her.

"Daisy," I said, "listen, honey, this jive is not going to get us any place. I am a musician and not a boxer. Every time you get mad at me the first thing you do is to try your damnedest to hit me in the chops. Thank the lord I have been able to get out of your way every time. Now I am sick and tired of it all. The best thing for me and you to do is call it quits."

"Oh, no. Don't leave me," Daisy said, breaking into tears. "You know I am in love with you. That's why I'm so jealous."

As I said before, Daisy did not have any education. If a person is real ignorant and has no learning at all that person is always going to be jealous, evil and hateful. There are always two sides to every story, but an ignorant person just won't cope with either side. I have seen Daisy get furious when she saw me whispering to somebody. "I know you are talking about me because you are looking at me," she would say. Frightening, isn't it? However, it was because I understood Daisy so well that I was able to take four years of torture and bliss with her.

A man has to know something or he will always catch hell. But Daisy did not even read a newspaper or anything enlightening. Luckily she was a woman, and a good-looking chick at that. Looks make all the difference in the world, no matter whether a woman is dumb or not. So we made it up and toughed it out together a little while longer.

At that time I was playing a lot of funerals with the Tuxedo Brass Band under the leadership of Oscar (Zost) Celestin, a marvelous trumpeter and a very fine musician. He was also one of the finest guys who ever hit New Orleans. I was the second trumpet player in his brass band. At the same time my dear friend Maurice Durand was playing in the Excelsior Brass Band, another top-notch band. Old Man Mauret was the leader and first cornet man, and he would pilot those musicians of his just as though they were a flock of angels. All his boys gave him wonderful support. They weren't like present day bands, only working because they have to, and mad because they have to take orders from the leader.

That was not true of Maurice and those other boys who played for Celestin and Old Man Mauret. Maurice and I were youngsters together. Whenever we played at a parade or a funeral we were usually playing in different bands. Lots of times I would run across Maurice and would see how wonderful Old Man Mauret's discipline was and how much his musicians appreciated him. Celestin was equally well loved by his musicians.

Since I am on the subject of first rate brass bands, I want to speak about the cream of the crop, the one that topped them all — the Onward Brass Band. On Labor Day and other holidays it was a thrilling experience to see the great King Oliver from Uptown and the past master Emmanuel Perez pass by blowing *Panama.* The memory of that is so wonderful that after all these years I would like nothing better than to be able to talk it all over again with Maurice, who is now living in San Francisco.

chapter 11

BY THIS TIME I was beginning to get very popular around that good old town of mine. I had many offers to leave Kid Ory's band, but for some time none of them tempted me. One day a redheaded band leader named Fate Marable came to see me. For over sixteen years he had been playing the excursion steamer *Sydney*. He was a great piano man and he also played the calliope on the top deck of the *Sydney*. Just before the boat left the docks for one of its moonlight trips up the Mississippi, Fate would sit down at this calliope and damn near play the keys off of it. He was certainly a grand musician.

When he asked me to join his orchestra I jumped at the opportunity. It meant a great advancement in my musical career because his musicians had to read music perfectly. Ory's men did not. Later on I found out that Fate Marable had just as many jazz greats as Kid Ory, and they were better men besides because they could read music and they could improvise. Fate's had a wide range and they played all the latest music because they could read at sight. Kid Ory's band could catch on to a tune quickly, and once they had it no one could outplay them. But I wanted to do more than fake the music all the time because there is more to music than just playing one style. I lost no time in joining the orchestra on the *Sydney*.

In that orchestra David Jones played the melophone. He had joined us from a road show that came to New Orleans, a fine musician with a soft mellow tone and a great ability to improvise. I mention him particularly because he took the trouble between trips to teach me to read music. I learned very quickly. Br'er Jones, as I later called him, taught me how to divide the notes so that whenever Fate threw a new arrangement I was able to cope with it, and did not have to sit and wait with my cornet in my hand for Joe Howard to play the tune once and then turn it over to me. Of course I could pick up a tune fast, for my ears were trained, and I could spell a little too, but not enough for Fate Marable's band.

Fate knew all this when he hired me, but he liked my tone and the way I could catch on. That was enough for him. Being a grand and experienced musician he knew that just by being around musicians who read music I would automatically learn myself. Within no time at all I was reading everything he put before me.

Fate was the kind of leader who liked to throw a hard piece of music at his boys and catch them off their guard. He would scan his part while the boys were out taking a smoke. After running his part down to perfection he would stamp his foot and say: "O.K. men. Here's your parts."

After the parts had been passed around he would stamp his foot again.

"Let's go," he would say.

Then we all scrambled to read the tune at first sight. By the time we were able to play our parts Fate had learned to play his without the notes. I thought that was marvelous. Fate was a very serious musician. He defied anybody to play more difficult music than he did. Every musician in New Orleans respected him. He had seen the good old days in Storyville, and had played cotch with the pimps and hustlers at the Twenty-Five gambling house. He had had fine jam sessions with the piano greats of those days such as Jelly Roll Morton, Tony Jackson, Calvin Jackson, Udell Wilson, Arthur Camel, Frankie Heinze, Boogus, Laurence Williams, Buddy Christian, Wilhelmina Bart Wynn, Edna Frances and many of the other all-time greats. He always won the greatest honors with them.

He had his own way of dealing with his musicians. If one of us made an error or played part of a piece wrong he would not say a thing about it until everyone thought it had been forgotten. When you came to work the next day with a bad hangover from the night before, he picked up the music you had failed with and asked you to play it before the other members of the band. And believe me, brother, it was no fun to be shown up before all the other fellows if you did not play that passage right; we used to call this experience our Waterloo. This was Fate's way of making his men rest properly so that they could work perfectly on the job the next night. I learned something from that, and to this day I still think it is good psychology.

When it was time for the steamer *Sydney* to leave New Orleans Fate Marable treated me very diplomatically. He knew I had never been out of the city in my whole life except to such small Louisiana small towns as Houma, West Wego, La Blaste (Ory's home town) and several other similar places. He wanted me to come with his band in the worst way. The older musicians, who idolized "Little Louis," told Fate he would be wasting his time even to try to get me to leave town. But Fate had a way of his own. He could see that I was very happy in his wonderful orchestra, playing the kind of music I had never played before in my life and piling up all the experiences I had dreamed of as an ambitious kid. He made me a feature man in his orchestra. I can still hear that fine applause I got from the customers.

What with David Jones giving me a helping hand in reading and Fate's strictness as a leader I had no desire by this time to leave the orchestra. Mind you, I was only with them for a try-out, or what they call an audition nowadays. Things were jumping so good for me that the minute Fate popped the question to me I said "yes" so fast that Fate could scarcely believe his ears.

When the boat docked that night after the moon-light ride I made a beeline to tell Daisy all about it, thinking she would be glad about my advancement. Instead of that she gave me a disgusted look as though she thought I was only leaving New Orleans to get rid of her. My feathers fell something awful. While I continued to talk about my good fortune she gave me a sickly grin and one of those forced kisses on the cheek.

"Are you going away and leave me all alone?" she asked.

"Well, Daisy darling," I said, "this is my one big chance to do the things I have been wanting to do all my life. If I turn this offer down the way I have been doing with others I'll be stuck here forever with nothing happening."

Then I used that old line about "opportunity only knocks once." With these words that chick's face brightened right up.

"Honey, I understand."

Then she gave me a real big kiss. And everything came out all right.

At the time I was too young to know all the ropes. I found out when we reached Saint Louis that I could have brought Daisy along.

Just before I left, Daisy and I went down on Canal Street to shop with the money I had been given as an advance on my salary. That was something that had never happened to me before. The only advance money we musicians ever got in those days was the deposits on the gigs we used to play. The only person who got that money was the contractor for the job or the leader of our little tail gate band. I never signed contracts for any of those jobs. That was done by Joe Lindsey, our drummer, who would keep all the deposits. The rest of us did not know enough to pay attention to what was going on. We were so glad to get a chance to blow our horns that nothing else mattered.

The only times we knew that money had been deposited in advance was when we had too many engagements in a night for us to be able to fill them all. Then people would come and demand that Joe return their money. Like fools we would back Joe up and play the job another day. New Orleans was famous for this sort of thing. From the big-shot band leaders such as Buddy Bolden, Joe Oliver, Bunk Johnson, Freddie Keppard and Emmanuel Perez, down to the kids of my age money was handled in this way.

That is one of the reasons I never cared to become a band leader; there was too much quarreling over petty money matters. I just wanted to blow my horn peacefully as I am doing now. I have always noticed that the band leader not only had to satisfy the crowd but that he also had to worry about the box office.

In addition to Fate, Joe Howard and myself, the other members of Marable's band when I joined were Baby Dodds, drums; George (Pops) Foster, bass; David Jones, melophone; Johnny St. Cyr, banjo guitar; Boyd

Atkins, swing violin, and another man whose name 1 have forgotten. Any kid interested in music would have appreciated playing with them, considering how we had to struggle to pay for lessons. Most of the time our parents could not pay fifty cents for a lesson. Things were hard in New Orleans in those days and we were lucky if we ate, let alone pay for lessons. In order to carry on at all we had to have the love of music in our bones.

The Streckfus Steam Boats were owned by four brothers, Vern, Roy, Johnny and Joe. Captain Joe was the oldest, and he was the big boss. There was no doubt about that. All of the brothers were fine fellows and they all treated me swell. At first I had the feeling that everybody was afraid of the big chief, Captain Joe. I had heard so much about how mean Captain Joe was that I could hardly blow my horn the first time I played on the steamer *Sydney*, but he soon put me at ease. But he did insist that everyone attend strictly to his business. When we heard he was coming on board everybody including the musicians would pitch in and make the boat spic and span. He loved our music; as he stood behind us at the bandstand he would smile and chuckle while he watched us swing, and he would order special tunes from us. We almost overdid it, trying to please him.

Captain Joe got the biggest boot out of Baby Dodds, our drummer, who used to shimmy while he beat the rim shots on his drum. Lots of times the whole boat would stop to watch him. Even after I stopped working on his boat Captain Joe used to bring his wife and family to hear me play my trumpet.

Captain Vern reminded me, smile and all, of my favorite movie comedian, Stan Laurel. At our very first meeting he gave me such a warm smile that I felt I had known him all my life. That feeling lasted as long as I was on that boat. Lots of people made a good living working on the boats of the Streckfus Line.

My last week in New Orleans while we were getting ready to go up river to Saint Louis I met a fine young white boy named Jack Teagarden. He came to New Orleans from Houston, Texas, where he had played in a band led by Peck Kelly. The first time I heard Jack Teagarden on the trombone I had goose pimples all over; in all my experience I had never heard anything so fine. Jack met all the boys in my band. Of course he met Captain Joe as well, for Captain Joe was a great music lover and he wanted to meet every good musician and have him play on one of his boats. Some of the finest white bands anyone could ever want to hear graced his bandstands, as well as the very best colored musicians. I did not see Jack Teagarden for a number of years after that first meeting, but I never ceased hearing about him and his horn and about the way he was improving all the time. We have been musically jammed buddies ever since we met.

Finally everything was set for me to leave my dear home town and travel up and down the lazy Mississippi River blowing my little old cornet from town to town. Fate Marable's Band deserves credit for breaking down a few barriers on the Mississippi — barriers set up by Jim Crow. We were the first colored band to play most of the towns at which we stopped, particularly the smaller ones. The ofays were not used to seeing colored boys blowing horns and making fine music for them to dance by. At first we ran into some ugly experiences while we were on the bandstand, and we had to listen to plenty of nasty remarks. But most of us were from the South anyway. We were used to that kind of jive, and we would just keep on swinging as though nothing had happened. Before the evening was over they *loved* us. We couldn't turn for them singing our praises and begging us to hurry back.

I will never forget the day I left New Orleans by train for Saint Louis to join the steamer *Saint Paul*. It was the first time in my life I had ever made a long trip by railroad. I had no idea as to what I should take, and my wife and mother did not either. For my lunch Mayann went to Prat's Creole Restaurant and bought me a great big fish sandwich and a bottle of green olives. David Jones, the melophone player in the band, took the same train with me. He was one of those erect guys who thought he knew everything. He could see that I was inexperienced, but he did not do anything to make the trip pleasant for me. He was older than I, and he had been traveling for years in road shows and circuses while I was in short pants.

When we arrived at Galesburg, Illinois, to change trains, my arms were full of all the junk I had brought with me. In addition to my cornet I had a beat-up suitcase which looked as though it had been stored away since Washington crossed the Delaware. In this grip (that's what we called a suitcase in those days) Mayann had packed all my clothes which I had kept at her house because Daisy and I quarrelled so much. The suitcase was so full there was not room for the big bottle of olives. I had to carry the fish sandwich and olives in one arm and the cornet and suitcase in the other. What a trip that was!

The conductor came through the train hollering: "All out for Galesburg." He followed this with a lot of names which did not faze me a bit, but when he said, "Change trains for Saint Louis," my ears pricked up like a jackass.

When I grabbed all my things I was so excited that I loosened the top of my olive bottle, but somehow I managed to reach the platform with my arms full. The station was crowded with people rushing in all directions. David Jones had had orders to look out for me, but he didn't. He was bored to tears. He acted as though I was just another colored boy he did not even know. That is the impression he tried to give people in the station. All of a sudden a big train came around the bend at what seemed to me a mile a minute. In the rush to get seats somebody bumped into me and knocked the olives out of my arm. The jar broke into a hundred pieces and the olives rolled all over the platform. David Jones immediately walked away and did not even turn around. I felt pretty bad about those good olives, but when I finally got on the train I was still holding my fish sandwich. Yes sir, I at least managed to keep that.

By this time I was getting kind of warm about Br'er Jones, and I went right up to him and told him off. I told him he put on too many airs and plenty more. And I did not say a word to him all the way to Saint Louis. There the laugh was on him. It was real cold and he was wearing an overcoat *and* a straw hat. When I heard the people roar with laughter as they saw David Jones get off the train I just laid right down on the ground and almost laughed myself to death. But his embarrassment was far worse than mine had been, and I finally began to feel sorry for him. He was a man of great experience and he should have known better. He could not get angry with me for laughing at him considering how he had treated me. Later on we became good friends, and that is when he started helping me out reading music.

The first night I arrived I was amazed by Saint Louis and its tall buildings. There was nothing like that in my home town, and I could not imagine what they were all for. I wanted to ask someone badly, but I was afraid I would be kidded for being so dumb. Finally, when we were going back to our hotel I got up enough courage to question Fate Marable.

"What are all those tall buildings? Colleges?"

"Aw boy," Fate answered, "don't be so damn dumb."

Then I realized I should have followed my first hunch and kept my mouth shut.

chapter 12

As the days rolled on I commenced getting hep to the jive. I learned a good deal about life and people as I shot dice with the waiters, the deck hands, the musicians and anybody else who gambled. Sometimes after we left the bandstand we would gamble all night and even up to the following night. Lots of times I would win, but most of the time I lost. Those waiters were old hustlers from 'way back, and so were the deck hands and musicians. Like everybody else I hated to lose, but since I was not used to having a whole lot of money — or even any money much of the time — I did not take my losses so hard as some of the more experienced fellows.

When we collected our pay I did not know what to buy so I bought a lot of cheap jive at the five and ten cents store to give to the kids in my neighborhood when I got back to New Orleans. I did not have to worry about Daisy and my mother because they both had good jobs. My sister Beatrice was down in Florida with her husband working on ome kind of saw mill job, and I did not have to send her anything either. So I ran from one salary to another spending money like water. I was the happiest kid musician in the world.

When I joined Fate's orchestra I weighed only one hundred and forty pounds. One day after I had been dissipating a lot I caught a cold. I asked David Jones to recommend something to cure it.

"Just get a bottle of Scott's Emulsion, and take it regularly until it is gone."

That is what I did, and within a week's time I had gained a great deal. As a matter of fact, when I got back to New Orleans I had to buy a pair of fat man's trousers. From that time on I never got back to my old fighting weight again. Of course, I got rid of that cold.

A funny thing happened on the steamer *Saint Paul* during an all day excursion. The boat was packed and jammed to the rafters and the band was swinging like mad. Between Alton and Quincy a young white boy made a bet with one of his buddies that he would jump off. The boy jumped and the deck hands shouted: "Man overboard. Man overboard!" Everybody ran to the side of the boat which suddenly began to list danger- ously. People did not quite realize what had happened and they rushed hollering and screaming all over the ship. It was a real panic. We musicians were on the stand blowing our heads off when the captain rushed up and shouted: "Keep playing. Keep playing." We played *Tiger Rag* until we were blue in the face and eventually most of the people quieted down.

The kid was a good swimmer, and he had almost reached the other side of the river when the captain sent a boat crew after him. He did not want to come back, and he put up a good fight before the boat crew could pull him in. Again the passengers rushed to the side to watch the excitement and again the boat started to list. "Keep on playing. Keep on playing," the captain con- tinued to shout. Finally the kid was brought back and locked up. The captain and some of the crew wanted to take a poke at him, but they realized he was only a child and had him arrested when the boat reached Saint Louis.

There were often fights on board during those trips, and almost everyone working on the ship would try to stop them. But the members of the band never did. We were colored, and we knew what that meant. We were not allowed to mingle with the white guests under any circumstances. We were there to play good music for them, and that was all. However, everybody loved us and our music and treated us royally. I and some of the other musicians in the band were from the South and we understood, so we never had any hard feelings. I have always loved my white folks, and they have always proved that they loved me and my music. I have never had anything to be depressed about in that respect, only respect and appreciation. Many a time white folks have invited me and my boys to the finest meals at their homes, with the best liquor you would want to smack your chops on — liquor I could not afford to buy.

I have been fortunate in working with musicians who did not drink too much when they were working. That can certainly cause a lot of trouble. I had my first experience when I started working in big time early in life. I had no idea how bad a guy can feel after a night of lushing. I was seventeen years old when my comrades carried me home to Mayann dead drunk. She was not bored with me at all, even though I was sick. After she had wrapped cold towels with ice in them around my head she put me to bed. Then she gave me a good physic and told the kids to go home.

"The physic will clean him out real good. After he has put one of my meals under his belt in the morning he'll be brand new."

Sure enough, that was just what happened.

My mother was always a quick thinker when she had to help people who were seriously sick. She came from a little town in Louisiana called Butte. Her parents had all been slaves, and she had been poor all her life. She had had to learn everything the hard way. My father was a common laborer who never had anything all his life. Mayann's parents could not afford doctors, and when any of the kids was sick they would gather herbs down by the railroad tracks. After these had been boiled down, the children drank them or rubbed their bodies with them. Believe me, the cure worked like magic. The sick kid was well in a jiffy and ready to start life over again.

I was so embarrassed to have Mayann see me drunk that I apologized again and again.

"Son," she told me, "you have to live your own life. Also you have to go out into this world all by your lone self. You need all the experiences you can get. Such as what's good and what's bad. I cannot tell you these things, you've got to see them for yourself. There's nobody in this world a better judge for what's good for your life than you. I would not dare scold you for taking a few nips. Your mother drinks all the liquor she wants. And I get pretty tight sometimes. Only I know how to carry my liquor to keep from getting sick."

Then she went on to explain to me what I should do if I got the urge again. She would not make me promise never to drink; I was too young to make such a resolution.

"Son," she added, "you don't know yourself yet. You don't know what you are going to want. I'll tell you what. Suppose you and I make all the honky-tonks one night? Then I can show you how to really enjoy good liquor."

"That would be fine, mama," I said. "That would be just grand, going out with my dear mother and having lots of fun together."

I felt like a real man, escorting a lady out to the swellest places in our neighborhood, the honky-tonks. All that week at work I looked forward to my night off. Then I could take Mayann out and she would show me how to hold my liquor.

Finally the night came, and I was loaded with cash. Those prosperous prostitutes who came to our joint would give us lots of tips to play different tunes for them and their "Johns." Sometimes the girls used to make their tricks give us money on general principles. The chicks liked to see their boys spend money since they could not get it for themselves all at once. Besides the chicks liked us personally.

On the night my mother and I went out cabareting we went first to Savocas' honky-tonk at Saratoga and Poydras Streets. This was the headquarters and also the pay office for the men working on the banana boats down at the levee. Lots of times I had stood in line there after working on those boats. And many times I went right in to the gambling table and lost my whole pay. But I didn't care — I wanted to be around the older fellows, the good old hustlers, pimps and musicians. I liked their language somehow.

Savocas' was known as one of the toughest joints in

the world, but I had been raised in the neighborhood and its reputation did not bother me at all. Everybody knew my mother and me. Mayann used to do washing and ironing for the hustling gals and the hustlers, and they paid well. On Saturday nights hustlers loved to wear their jumpers and overalls to hustle in. The jumper is like a blue coat; overalls were like what we call dungarees. The hustlers thought this outfit brought good luck to them and their whores.

When the girls were hustling they would wear real short dresses and the very best of silk stockings to show off their fine, big legs. They all liked me because I was little and cute and I could play the kind of blues they liked. Whenever the gals had done good business they would come into the honky-tonk in the wee hours of the morning and walk right up to the bandstand. As soon as I saw them out of the corner of my eye I would tell Boogus, my piano man, and Garbee, my drummer man, to get set for a good tip. Then Boogus would go into some good old blues and the gals would scream with delight.

As soon as we got off the bandstand for a short intermission the first gal I passed would say to me: "Come here, you cute little son of a bitch, and sit on my knee."

Hmmmm! You can imagine the effect that had on a youngster like me. I got awfully excited and hot under the collar. "I am too young," I said to myself, "to even come near satisfying a hard woman like her. She always has the best of everything. Why does she pick on me? She has the best pimps." (I always felt inferior to the pimps.)

I was always afraid of the hustling gals because of my experience with the chick who pulled her bylow knife on me and stabbed me in the shoulder. Still the whores continued to chase me. Of course I must admit I just couldn't resist letting some of the finer ones catch up with me once in a while.

However, let's get back to the night Mayann and I went out sporting 'em up. After we left Savocas' we went to Spanol's tonk around the corner. As soon as we entered everybody gave us a big hello.

"Where you been keeping yourself?" they all asked Mayann. "You are a sight for sore eyes."

Then they all shouted: "Mother and son are making the rounds tonight. We all ought to have good luck."

"Give me a twenty dollar card," one of the big-shot gamblers hollored to the game keeper. "I feel very, very lucky tonight."

Mother and I did not have a chance to spend much money that night. Everybody kept pouring whiskey down into our stomachs. It was the first time they had ever seen us together.

All the time Mayann kept explaining to me how to hold my liquor. I took it all in and said "Yes, mom's" to everything she told me. I was anxious to learn everything I could. At my boss' joint Henry Matranga asked us to have a drink on the house.

[199]

"You have a fine boy," he told Mayann. "He is well liked by everybody who comes to my place. We all predict he will be a very fine musician some day. His heart is in it."

Mayann poked out her chest with pride.

"Thank God for that," she said. "I was never able to give my son a decent education like he deserved. I could see he had talent within him from a wee youngster. But I could not do very much about it, except just pray to the Lord to guide him and help him. And the Lord has answered my prayers greatly. Am I proud of my boy? God in heaven knows I am. And many thanks to you, Mr. Matranga, for letting him work at your place, knowing he did not have the experience he needed. But you tolerated him just the same and the Lord will bless you for it. I shall remember you every night when I say my prayers. With all you people pulling for Louis, the way you all are doing, he just can't miss."

Just then Slippers, the bouncer, came into the bar and yelled: "Hello, Mayann. What in the world are you doing out on the stroll tonight?"

When she told him we were making the rounds he thought it was the cutest thing he had seen in a long time. Then he insisted that we have a drink with him.

By this time my mother and I were getting pretty tight, and we had not visited even half of the joints. But we were determined to make them all; that was our agreement and we intended to stick to it. Besides we were both having a fine time meeting the people who loved us and spoke our language. We knew we were among our people. That was all that mattered. We did not care about the outside world.

Slippers, who should have been in the back room keeping an eye on the bad men, stayed on at the bar with us. He just had to tell Mayann how good I was on that quail.

"Mayann, that boy of yours should really go up North and play with the good horn blowers."

"Thanks, Slippers," Mayann said, downing another drink and stuttering slightly. "Thanks, Slippers. You know . . . I'm proud of that boy. He's all I got. He and his sister, Mama Lucy. Of course his no good father has never done anything decent for those children. Only their stepfathers. Good thing they had good stepfathers, or else I don't know what those two children would have done."

Mayann downed another drink, and just as she did somebody in the back room shouted:

"Slippers! Slippers. Come real quick. There's a bad man from out of town who won't pay off his debts."

Slippers made one leap to the rear. In less than no time he was running the guy to the door by the seat of his pants. He gave him a punch on the chops, saying: "Get the hell out of here, you black son of a bitch, and don't come back again, ever."

That was that. Nobody dared to mess around with Slippers. He was a good man with a pistol and he knew how to handle his dukes. He could fight fair and he could fight dirty, whichever his victim preferred. But he was as nice a fellow as God ever made. I loved him just as though he had been my father. Whenever I was around fellows like Slippers or Black Benny I felt secure. Just to be in their company was like heaven to me.

After the guy had been thrown out we finished our drinks. At least we tried to finish them for they were lined up like soldiers. We said good night to Matranga and the crowd and were on our merry way to Joe Segretta's at Liberty and Perdido, the street that became so famous that Duke Ellington wrote a tune about it.

Segretta served extract of Jamaica ginger for fifteen cents a bottle. Everybody was buying this jive and adding it to half a glass of water, so Mayann and I joined in. That drink gave you just what you would expect; it knocked you flat on your tail. I could see that Mayann's eyes were getting glassy but she still asked me: "Son, are you all right?"

"Sure, mother. I'm having lots of fun."

"Whenever you get ready to go home just let me know and we will cut out."

For some reason or other I was fresh as a daisy. From the way I was holding up you would have sworn I was immune to the lush. Mother and I had two of those bottles of Jamaica ginger each, and by that time it was getting real late. I could see that mother was getting soused, but I did not want to go home without stopping at Henry Ponce's place across the street. He, as you know, was the good-looking Frenchman of the old Storyville days, and Joe Segretta's competitor. Joe would have rather been bitten by a tiger than see Henry Ponce walk the streets.

Henry Ponce thought a good deal of me and I admired him too. I used to love to see those real beautiful women of all colors who came to the Third Ward especially to see him. Of course they did not like the neighborhood he was in, after he had been run out of Storyville, but they loved him. These women used to tip us plenty to play the tunes they liked. There is no doubt about it, Ponce was a mighty man. When you are talking about real operators who really played it cool, think of Henry Ponce.

The minute mother and I stepped into his joint he spied me and ran out from behind the bar to greet me. He did not know Mayann, so I introduced her.

"I am so very glad to meet you," Ponce said right away. "You are the mother of a real good boy. He has nice manners, he works with all his heart and he has never given me an ounce of trouble. I am certainly glad to meet you. Your boy is ambitious and he is anxious to get somewhere. I watched him closely when he was working for me from eight in the evening to four in the morning. I knew that he used to work all day long at the coal yard. I could not understand how he could

[203]

keep it up. He is serious about his career, I want you to understand that."

The bartender brought us a round of drinks and we downed these too. Then the three pieces which had replaced our band started jumping a tune and Mayann and I danced. I noticed she was yawning, but I did not say a word.

After the dance was over we went back to our table to finish our drink. When we got up to go, Mayann started over to say good night to Henry Ponce. She was weaving a little and after she had taken a half dozen steps she fell flat on her face. Not realizing I had had as many as she, I went over to pick her up. As I leaned over I fell right on top of her. Everybody in the place broke out laughing. My mother had a good sense of humor, drunk or sober, and she joined in with the laughter. Everybody was in stitches, including me.

Stepfather Gabe was standing across the street at Joe Segretta's corner. When he had gone home he had found we were out and he was looking for us when somebody told him to go over to Ponce's place. When he saw what had happened he joined in the laughter and picked us up. He straightened Mayann's hat and hair as best he could, and led us to the door with a big smile on his face for everybody. He stopped to shake hands with Ponce and tell him what a swell gentleman he was. He thanked him for giving me a chance to play when an older musician would have given better service. Ponce told Gabe that an older musician did not have what this youngster had — sincerity and a kind of creative power which the world would eventually recognize. Gabe did not understand all those big words, but he thanked Ponce and went out supporting both mother and me with his strong arms.

When we started going down the street toward home, which was not over a block away, it was about daybreak and there were only a few stragglers on the street. We were weaving badly as we walked and we pulled Mr. Gabe from one side of the sidewalk to the other as we lurched. Any of the passers-by who saw us must have thought Gabe was as drunk as Mayann and me. However, he was very good natured about the whole business.

"Son," Mayann said, "I am convinced that you know how to hold your liquor. Judging by what happened last night you can take care of yourself. I feel that I have found out just what I wanted to know. You can look out for yourself if anything happens to me."

I felt very proud of myself.

I have told about this night with mother in connection with what I was saying about musicians who do not get drunk while they are working. Now I want to tell about a bad experience on the *Saint Paul* one summer night in an Iowa town. We had been going up and down the river for days giving one-nighters at every town at which we stopped. We reached this place in Iowa early in the day so we had a chance to go ashore and look around. This was unusual because we generally pulled out after each moonlight excursion and were sailing all day long.

On this particular day Baby Dodds ran into some old pals who took him to a house where there was loads of liquor. Baby forgot he had to work that night and he drank a good deal too much. Everybody who knew Baby knew that when he started drinking the best thing to do was to clear out. That is, if you liked him too much to want to hurt him.

That night he was not satisfied to reach the boat late. When he got to the bandstand he reeled over to the drums while the crowd of white folks watched. To try to cover things up leader Fate Marable immediately went into a number. We all of us blew like mad to try to hide Dodd's blunders. We did the best to help our boy out although he was dragging the tempo something awful. The boys were all mad as hell but they tried to make the best of a bad situation. Finally Baby got insulted and started calling us a gang of black bastards. This did not matter to us, but the customers heard it. That was another matter.

Fate called intermission which we usually spent on the power deck where you can watch the water as the boat rolls along. Fate called Baby and tried to talk to him. He thought it was far better for him to try to calm Baby down than to have a white man butt in. But he did not succeed. Baby began to get louder and to swear more. This is where I came in. I was a very dear friend of Baby, and I had had a lot of success with him in other scrimmages. I felt sure that as soon as I asked him to come with me and talk it over he would do so. Then I could at least protect him until the night's work was over.

Baby had just said that he was going to bust someone in the nose. I jumped in front of him.

"Look here, Baby, don't say that. You wouldn't hit anybody."

"You're damn right I would," he said.

"You wouldn't hit me, would'ja?" I said expecting him to say no.

Instead he said: "I'll hit you and I'll hit the boss."

Well sir, you could have bought me for a dime. I just took my little self off and sat down in a corner while Baby kept on raving and swearing like mad. Suddenly Captain Johnny, one of the Streckfus brothers and a huge brawny fellow, came over and asked Baby nicely to stop swearing. All the women and children aboard could hear him. To my surprise Baby told Captain Johnny where to go and what to do. "God help Baby!" I thought. Captain Johnny grabbed him by the neck with his two powerful hands and began to choke him until he was red in the face.

Baby had been bulldozing us plenty, but he was as tame as a lamb now. It was a gruesome sight. Everybody stood around in a cold sweat, but nobody said "Don't choke him any more" or ask for mercy. We were too tense and too sore at Baby to say a word. Baby sank to his knees and Captain Johnny released him as he passed out.

We had to go back to the bandstand and play without Dodds. Then Fate went to Captain Johnny and asked him to forgive the whole thing. Finally, thank God, the night was over. It was the worst and most painful drunken scene I had ever witnessed. Nowadays, however, Baby and I can laugh about it whenever we meet.

It was a useful experience for me to work on the boat with all those big-shots in music. From some of them I learned valuable methods of playing, from others I learned to guard against acquiring certain nasty traits. I was interested in their way of handling money. David Jones, for instance, starved himself the whole summer we worked on the *Saint Paul*. He saved every nickel and sent all his money to a farm down South where employees and relatives were raising cotton for him and getting away with as much of his money as they could, since he was not there to look after his own interests. Every day he would eat an apple instead of a good hot meal. What was the result? The boll weevils ate all of his cotton before the season was over. He did not even have a chance to go down and look his farm over before a telegram came saying everything had been shot to hell. After that David Jones used to stand at the boat rail during every intermission looking down at the water and thinking about all the jack he had lost. I often said to Fate Marable:

"Fate, keep an eye on David Jones. He's liable to jump in the water most any minute."

This incident taught me never to deprive my stomach. As a kid I had never believed in "cutting off my nose to spite my face," which is a true expression if there ever was one. I'll probably never be rich, but I will be a fat man. I never deprived myself of things I thought absolutely necessary, and there are a lot of things I never cared for, such as a flock of suits, for example. I have seen fellows with as many as twenty-five or thirty suits at one time. And what good does that do? The moths eat them up before they can get full use out of them. I have just the number of suits I need, including my uniforms. I have always believed in giving a hand to the underdog whenever I could, and as a rule I could. I will continue to do so as long as I live, and I expect to live a long, long time. Way past the hundred mark.

After the first trip to Saint Louis we went up river to Davenport, Iowa, where all the Streckfus boats put up for the winter. It was there that I met the almighty Bix Beiderbecke, the great cornet genius. Every musician in the world knew and admired Bix. He made the greatest reputation possible for himself, and we all respected him as though he had been a god. Whenever we saw him our faces shone with joy and happiness, but long periods would pass when we did not see him at all.

At the end of the first season on the *Saint Paul*

we played our last engagement at Saint Louis for a moonlight excursion for colored people. The boat was crowded to the rafters. After we were under way a quarrel broke out and some bad men from uptown pulled guns. Wow! I never in all my life saw so many colored people running every which way. "This is going to be worse than the scare we had when the lad jumped overboard," I said to myself. Again the captain gave orders to us to keep playing, and again I started looking for an exit. It was real tough that night, but the boat finally landed safely, and very few were hurt.

After we were through playing we went uptown to our hotels. On our way we could hear guys on every corner bragging about the way they had raised hell on the boat. "My goodness," I thought, "that may be their idea of having fun, but it certainly isn't my idea of a good time."

At the Grand Central Hotel in St. Louis I was a very popular boy. Being the youngest fellow in Fate Marable's band and single too, all the maids made a lot of fuss over me. I thought I was hot stuff when the gals argued over me, saying "I saw him first" and "He's my man" and a lot of blah like that. I was too interested in my music to pay any attention to that sort of jive. To most of it anyway.

chapter 13

WHEN THE SEASON ENDED at Davenport, Iowa, Captain Joe Streckfus gave each one of us his bonus, which consisted of all the five dollars kept out of our pay each week during the whole season. That was a nice taste of money, especially to a guy like me who was not used to loot that came in big numbers. I was heavily loaded with dough when I returned to New Orleans. The Streckfus people had given us our fare back and money to eat with on the trip. They were real swell people, those Streckfus boys. Each year I worked for them I felt more and more like a member of the family.

When I reached New Orleans I went straight away

to Liberty and Perdido, the corner where I used to hang out before I was lucky enough to find the job with Fate Marable. The first person I ran into was Black Benny standing at the bar in Joe Segretta's saloon with a few old-timers.

"Well I'll be damned," he said as I walked in, "if it ain't old Dipper."

He did not take his eyes off me as I walked up, and he kept on loudtalking me.

"Come heah you little sonofabitch. You been up North blowing dat horn o' your'n. I know you're sticking."

He meant he knew I had plenty of money. He asked me to stand him to a drink, and who was I to refuse the great Black Benny a drink? Nobody else ever did. When the drinks came I noticed that everybody had ordered. I threw down a twenty dollar bill to pay for the round which cost about six or seven bucks. When the bartender counted out my change Black Benny immediately reached for it saying, "I'll take it." I smiled all over my face. What else could I do? Benny wanted the money and that was that. Besides I was so fond of Benny it did not matter anyway. I do believe, however, if he had not strong armed that money out of me I would have given him lots more. I had been thinking about it on the train coming home from St. Louis. But since Benny did it the hard way I gave the idea up. I sort of felt he should have treated me like a man, and I did not like the way he cut under me. But I did not want to jump him up about it. That would have been just like putting my big head in the lion's mouth. So I disgustedly waited for an opening to leave, and did.

When I got home Daisy was waiting for me with a big pot of red beans and rice. She gave me a big kiss which sure did taste good. Then I had to sit down and tell her all about my trip — how nice it was, how nice everybody was to me and how everybody enjoyed my music immensely. She was so happy to hear it all that she swooned and carried on no end. All the time I was thinking to myself: "Hmmm. If Daisy would only always be as sweet to me as she is today. If only we would never have another fight and try to tear down the house we strived so hard to build, life would be oh so sweet."

We were so glad to see each other that we kissed and kissed and kissed some more. I had been away from her for six months, and it was the first time I had been so far away from home. Even when I was living with mother I would not go that far away, even though I received quite a few offers to go to different places to play my trumpet. Of course in those early days we did not know very much about trumpets. We all played cornets. Only the big orchestras in the theaters had trumpet players in their brass sections.

It is a funny thing, but at that time we all thought you had to be a music conservatory man or some kind of a big muckity-muck to play the trumpet. For years I would not even try to play the instrument.

After I had spent a few days at home with Daisy, Mayann naturally insisted that I come to dinner with her, my sister and Clarence. That dinner was a real problem. Since she had raised all three of us, she knew what big appetites we had. If she invited "the wrecking crew," as she called us, she would have to put on the big pot and the little one. She would have to go to Rampart Street and figure out what she could get the mostest of with the little money she had.

She went to Zatteran's grocery, and bought a pound of red beans, a pound of rice, a big slice of fat back and a big red onion. At Stahle's bakery she got two loaves of stale bread for a nickel. She boiled this jive down to a gravy, and I'll tell you that when we came we could smell her pot almost a block away. Mayann could really cook.

When Mama Lucy, Clarence and I sat down to the table we needed a lot of elbow room so as not to get in each other's way. After two encores I had to get up from the table for fear I would hurt myself. Clarence had one of the finest appetites I have ever seen in a kid. When I was young I was content with bread and butter or a slice of dry bread — it did not matter much so long as I was eating something. But Clarence was different, and I used to have a lot of fun with him when we sat down to table together.

"Well, son," I said that day at Mayann's, "I am going to eat more than you can."

"It's O.K. by me, Pops."

From then on it was perpetual motion, with Clarence far out ahead. Mama Lucy was not doing so bad, but in such fast company as Clarence and I she was nowhere. My mother just stood by and watched us with pride. She loved to see us eat a lot. That is why she worked so hard in the white folks' yards, washing, ironing and taking care of the white kids.

When I was not playing on the boat I used to take odd jobs. In 1921, the last year I was on the boat, I went to work at Tom Anderson's cabaret on Rampart between Canal and Iberville. That was a swell job if there ever was one. Only the richest race-horse men came to Anderson's. They spent a lot of money, and they gave us lots of tips to play tunes for them and their chicks. They would order big meals and just mince over them. Since I was a dear friend of all the colored waiters they gave me a break. When they would pass the bandstand on the way to the kitchen with the dead soldiers, or leftovers, they would look me in the eye and I would give them the well known wink. During intermission I would head straight for the kitchen and all the fine food that was waiting for me. What meals those were! The best steaks, chickens, chops, quail and many other high priced dishes. I felt real important eating all those fine meals, meals I could not have possibly paid for then, or even today.

The leader of our four piece combination at Anderson's was Paul Dominguez, a very fine Creole musician. I think he stood toe to toe with the best of them in those days. I will even go further and say that he was a little more modern than the others. And we had some very good musicians at the time. Among them were A. J. Piron, Peter Bocage, John Robechaux, and Emile Bigard, the uncle of Barney Bigard, our clarinet man. There was also Jimmy Paalow, who left New Orleans in 1915 when we were all in short pants with Keppard's Creole Jazz Band. That was the first band to leave New Orleans and make good. Of course there were lots of other good fiddlers, but for me Paul Dominguez was the best, and it was a pleasure to work for him. He was a sympathetic and understanding leader, and he was not a sore head like some of the leaders I have worked under at various times.

At Tom Anderson's we had a big kitty in front of the bandstand into which customers could drop "something" every time they requested a tune. We made more on tips than on our salary. Mr. Anderson was not seen around the place much, but his manager, George Delsa, was there every night. He reminded me of Costello of the team Abbott and Costello.

In Paul Dominguez' little four piece orchestra Albert Frances played the drums, his wife Edna the piano, and I the cornet. Later on Wilhelmina Bert Wynn replaced Edna when she became pregnant. Both of these girls were much better than a number of the men I have heard through the years.

I might have made — or lost — a lot of dough if

I had been interested in the horses. Several of the big-shot jockey and race track betters used to try to stet on the horses after I had played a request for them. But I was too wrapped up in music to try my luck on the race track. I would thank them very, very much and forget the whole business in a good jam session.

Among the other cabarets in New Orleans while I was working for Tom Anderson were The Cadillac, The Pup and Butsy Fernandez' place. All were jumping good music. When Anderson closed down for repairs, Zutty Singleton, who worked at Butsy's with the fine piano man Udell Wilson, hired me to play with them. We were a red hot trio and musicians would come in to our place every night after they had finished work. Most of them would sit in with us.

I will never forget the night Baby Dodds dropped in to see us after he had come off the road. We introduced him to our boss Butsy. Butsy, by the way, was the sharpest dressed man in New Orleans. He was also a great dancer. The night Rudolph Valentino was in New Orleans during a tour of the United States Butsy won the Rudolph Valentino prize for dancing. He was so sharp that night that all the women made a charge for him. I do believe Butsy was one of the nicest fellows alive. Except for Joe Glaser who was, and still is, the nicest boss man I've ever worked for.

To return to Baby Dodds, he decided to sit in with us that night and play on Zutty's drums. Zutty had struggled hard to pay for those drums. When Baby sat down to do his stuff he romped and played so loud and hard that before we realized it he had busted a hole clean through one of the drums. I never saw Zutty so mad in all my life. All Baby said was: "I'm sorry."

By closing time Baby and Zutty were about to come to blows. Much as I hate to interfere in fights, I had to step between them. They were both my boys, particularly Zutty, and I did not want anything to happen to him. Not that he could not have taken care of himself, but I just did not want those boys to fight.

After that night Zutty and Baby never felt the same about each other. Zutty and all the rest of us felt that Baby had acted badly. There was no reason why a musician with his big reputation could not have played the drums with a little more finesse.

Zutty and I stayed with Butsy until business began to get bad. Then it was the usual thing: no biz, no pay. We stood as many salary cuts as we could, and then we cut out.

Things were rather slow all during the year 1921. My last season on the excursion boats gave me a few dollars to skate along on until something decent turned up. What with playing parades, funerals and picnics for white folks, I did pretty well financially.

Toward the end of 1921 I became a permanent, full-fledged member of the Tuxedo Brass Band under the leadership of the trumpet player Celestin. I really felt that I was somebody. I also realized one of my greatest ambitions: to play second cornet to the one and only Joe Oliver, who had been named "King"

Oliver after making such a wonderful reputation in Chicago in 1918.

That Tuxedo Brass Band was really something, both to see and to hear, and it is too bad that in those days we did not have tape recorders and movie cameras to record those boys in action. Still we could not have bought those gadgets. We needed all the dough we could get to eat with.

When I played with the Tuxedo Brass Band I felt just as proud as though I had been hired by John Philip Sousa or Arthur Pryor. It was a great thrill when they passed out the brass band music on stiff cards that could be read as you walked along. I took great pains to play my part right and not miss a note. If I made a mistake I was brought down the whole day, but Celestin quickly saw how interested I was in my music. He appreciated that. When he thought something in the music might stump me he would come over to me and say:

"Son, are you all right? Can you manage that?"

That was a good deal of encouragement for a young fellow without too much brass band experience. I am still grateful to Papa Celestin as well as to all the members of his band who were always very pleasant to me.

The Tuxedo Brass Band had the same kind of summer uniform as the Onward Brass Band: white band caps with black trimmings, blue shirts, white pants and tan shoes. Since the Onward Brass Band had broken up, we came into power. Fine as they were, the other brass bands took their hats off to us.

The fact that I belonged to the best brass band in town put me in touch with all the top musicians. One of them was Picou, the finest clarinetist in New Orleans. He adapted the piccolo part in *High Society* to the clarinet, and whenever that piece is played the clarinetist uses Picou's solo. There were a number of other masters on the clarinet such as Tio, Bechet, Sidney Desvigne, Sam Dutrey, Wade Whaley and young Jim Williams, Jr. Williams died young and the world really lost a great musician. The same thing is true about Rappolo, who also died young. Other clarinet greats were Bill Humphrey, Johnny Dodds, Jimmy Noone and Albert Nicholas. Barney Bigard came along later, but he was equal to the best of them in my estimation. Since I am talking about old-timers I must not fail to mention Lawrence Dewey, who was a good man in his day. He has retired to Lafayette, Louisiana, but he still plays occasional odd jobs. He did a lot of work with the one and only Bunk Johnson. Louis Warner and Charlie McCurtis were also very good clarinet men.

No matter how long I live and no matter how many other musicians I play with I won't meet any better men than those I mention here. I had a chance to really dig them. The older and the younger men all put their souls into their work. The youngsters of those days, like me, took their music far more seriously than the present day ones. They were so superior to the beginners now that no comparison is possible.

Take for example George Backet who used to play a little E-flat cornet in the Excelsior Brass Band. Backet could be heard blocks away above the whole band. When he played his soulful lead with the other cornets, but an octave higher, he would actually bring tears to your eyes.

There are many other good clarinet men I could praise, but after all this time I cannot remember their names. I was real young when I played with them, and we did not bother much about correct names in those days. We used such nicknames as Gate, Face and Gizzard when we said hello or good-bye. As a rule we would meet on a gig, or one night stand, and we would play so well together that one would swear we had been working in the same outfit for months.

In the same year of 1921 Daisy adopted a little girl called Wila Mae Wilson. At this time we had moved out to the white neighborhood at Saint Charles and Clio Streets in the rear of the white folk's home where Daisy worked. To get to our place we had to go through a rear alley, and I was rather afraid when I came home in the wee hours of the night that I might be taken for a burglar. And as a matter of fact, that is what did happen. I had finished working about four o'clock in the morning. When I got off the streetcar to go toward my alley I noticed an old white fellow coming toward me about half a block away. He came closer to me as I neared the alley. Something told me not to enter. The fellow seemed suspicious of me so I waited at the entrance to the alley. When he reached me and was about to pass by I spoke to him. He stopped.

"Listen here," I said, "you may think I am up to something. But I want you to know that I live in this alley. My wife works for some white folks and we're staying on the premises. I thought I'd mention this so's you won't start no stuff."

"I'm sure glad you told me," the old geezer said, "because I am the watchman around here and I don't recall ever seeing you. O.K., go ahead. I'll watch out for you from now on."

He could have saved his breath. The minute I got in the house I wakened Daisy and Wila Mae out of a sound sleep, and told them we would have to move away at daybreak. Then I told them what had happened, and Daisy gave her notice in the morning. I found three rooms at Saratoga and Erato.

Cute little thirteen-year-old Wila Mae did not care where we moved so long as we took her with us. Her mother had brought Wila Mae and her sister Violet from a small Louisiana town. Violet, who was fourteen, died very young. Wila Mae lived with Daisy even after I went North to join King Oliver at the Lincoln Gardens in Chicago in 1922. She became a very fine young lady, and before we knew what had happened she married a boy named Sibley and had a son she called Archie.

The people in New Orleans knew me as Wila Mae's godfather, and when her son grew old enough to know what it was all about he became as fond of me as he was of his mother. Then I became his godfather too. He even took up the trumpet because of me and changed his name to Archie Armstrong, a name that will be his the rest of his life.

Daisy grew so fond of Wila Mae that I was surprised. Daisy never did take to anybody very much. Lots of times she did not care very much even for me. But she loved me and I loved her, and that was that. I can go so far as to say that she was true to me all the time we lived together. When I left for Chicago we were spatting, and I was not responsible for anybody she went with after that. Later I found out that she was running around New Orleans with a childhood friend of mine named Shots Madison. He also was a good cornet player, so everybody said that Daisy only fell for cornet players. After all, a cornet is not a bad instrument to fall for.

My sister Mama Lucy went back to the little sawmill town in Florida where she lived with her old man, her common law husband, for many years. They ran a little gambling joint down there and made all kinds of money. Many times I felt like asking them to lay a little loot on me, but I never did. I have always felt that no matter how much money your relatives may be making they have not got any more than they need. As the good book says, it is better to give than to receive. I would always delight in giving my family as much money as I could, but I dreaded asking them for anything. I was always the lucky one when it came to making money. In my early music days, of course, I did not make an awful lot, but at that I made a little more money than fellows who did not have any profession at all.

In my neighborhood everybody was a little frightened when they heard Lucy was dealing cards and running a game among bad characters. I told them not to worry about her. Mama Lucy was not afraid of bad men. She always kept her chib handy, and with that wide long blade she would soon carve up anybody who tried to get out of line.

There are two women with whom I always felt perfectly safe when they had their chibs with them: sister Mama Lucy and my wife Daisy. It is a funny thing, but hot headed and quick tempered as Daisy was, she never tried to carve me with her knife. Of course several times we had a brick throwing contest, but that was just part of the New Orleans tradition which I had known since I was a kid. I knew well enough how to keep from being hit. Daisy could give Don Newcomb an awful race throwing a curve with a brick. But for all that it did not stop my love for her and for my cornet.

All the big, well known Social Aid and Pleasure Clubs turned out for the last big parade I saw in New Orleans. They all tried to outdo each other and they certainly looked swell. Among the clubs represented were The Bulls, The Hobgoblins, The Zulus, The Tammanys, The Young Men Twenties (Zutty Singleton's club), The Merry-Go-Rounds, The Deweys, The Tulane Club, The Young Men Vidalias, The Money Wasters, The Jolly Boys, The Turtles, The Original

Swells, The San Jacintos, The Autocrats, The Frans
Sa Mee Club, The Cooperatives, The Economys, The
Odd Fellows, The Masons, The Knights of Pythias
(my lodge), and The Diamond Swells from out in the
Irish Channel. The second liners were afraid to go into
the Irish Channel which was that part of the city located
uptown by the river front. It was a dangerous neighborhood. The Irish who lived out there were bad men,
and the colored boys were tough too. If you followed
a parade out there you might come home with your
head in your hand.

To watch those clubs parade was an irresistible
and absolutely unique experience. All the members
wore full dress uniforms and with those beautiful silk
ribbons streaming from their shoulders they were a
magnificent sight. At the head of the parade rode the
aides, in full dress suits and mounted on fine horses
with ribbons around their heads. The brass band
followed, shouting a hot swing march as everyone
jumped for joy. The members of the club marched
behind the band wearing white felt hats, white silk
shirts (the very best silk) and mohair trousers. I had
spent my life in New Orleans, but every time one of
those clubs paraded I would second-line them all day
long. By carrying the cornet for Joe Oliver or Bunk
Johnson I would get enough to eat to hold me until
the parade was over.

When a club paraded it would make several stops
called "punches" during the day at houses of the members, where there were sandwiches, cold beer and, of

course, lots of whiskey. The whiskey did not interest me at that time. All I wanted was to be allowed to hang around with the fellows.

When all the clubs paraded it took nearly all day to see them pass, but one never got tired watching. Black Benny was always the star attraction. He was the only man, musician or not, who dared to go anywhere, whether it was the Irish Channel, Back o' Town, the Creole section in the Seventh Ward or any other tough place. Nobody would have the nerve to bother him. He was just that tough and he was not afraid of a living soul. Wherever he went outside of our ward to beat the drums or to dance he was always treated with the greatest respect.

By the year 1922 I had become so popular from playing in Kid Ory's band and the Tuxedo Brass Band that I too could go into any part of New Orleans without being bothered. Everybody loved me and just wanted to hear me blow, even the tough characters were no exception. The tougher they were the more they would fall in love with my horn, just like those good old hustlers during the honky-tonk days.

Joe Oliver had left New Orleans in 1918, and was now up in Chicago doing real swell. He kept sending me letters and telegrams telling me to come up to Chicago and play second cornet for him. That, I knew, would be real heaven for me.

I had made up my mind that I would not leave New Orleans unless the King sent for me. I would not risk leaving for anyone else. I had seen too many of my little pals leave home and come back in bad shape. Often their parents had to send them the money to come back with. I had had such a wonderful three years on the excursion boats on the Mississippi that I did not dare cut out for some unknown character who might leave me stranded or get me into other trouble. Fate Marable and the Streckfus brothers had made it impossible for me to risk spoiling everything by running off on a wild goose chase.

After I had made all my arrangements I definitely accepted Joe's offer. The day I was leaving for Chicago I played at a funeral over in Algiers, on August 8, 1922. The funeral was for the father of Eddie Vincent, a very good trombone player. When the body was brought out of the house to go to the cemetery the hymn we played was *Free as a Bird*, and we played it so beautifully that we brought tears to everybody's eyes.

The boys in the Tuxedo Brass Band and Celestin's band did their best to talk me out of going up to Chicago. They said that Joe Oliver was scabbing and that he was on the musicians' union's unfair list. I told them how fond I was of Joe and what confidence I had in him. I did not care what he and his band were doing. He had sent for me, and that was all that mattered. At that time I did not know very much about union tactics because we did not have a union in New Orleans, so the stuff about the unfair list was all Greek to me.

When the funeral was over I rushed home, threw my few glad rags together and hurried over to the

[227]

Illinois Central Station to catch the seven p. m. train for the Windy City. The whole band came to the station to see me off and wish me luck. In a way they were all glad to see me get a chance to go out in the world and make good, but they did not care so much about having me play second cornet to Joe Oliver. They thought I was good enough to go on my own, but I felt it was a great break for me even to sit beside a man like Joe Oliver with all his prestige.

It seemed like all of New Orleans had gathered at the train to give me a little luck. Even the old sisters of my neighborhood who had practically raised me when I was a youngster were there. When they kissed me good-bye they had handkerchiefs at their eyes to wipe away the tears.

When the train pulled in all the pullman porters and waiters recognized me because they had seen me playing on the tail gate wagons to advertise dances, or "balls" as we used to call them. They all hollered at me saying, "Where are you goin', Dipper?"

"You're a lucky black sommitch," one guy said, "to be going up North to play with ol' Cocky."

This was a reference to the cataract on one of Joe's eyes. The mean guys used to kid him about his bad eye, and he would get fighting mad. But what was the use? If he had messed around fighting with those guys he would have ended up by losing his good eye.

When the conductor hollered all aboard I told those waiters: "Yeah man, I'm going up to Chicago to play with my idol, Papa Joe! "

chapter 14

WHEN I GOT ON THE TRAIN I found an empty seat next to a lady and her three children, and she was really sticking. What I mean by "sticking" is that she had a big basket of good old southern fried chicken which she had fixed for the trip. She had enough to last her and her kids not only to Chicago, but clear out to California if she wanted to go that far.

I hit the fish sandwich Mayann had prepared for me, but at the same time I was trying my darnedest to think of something to say that would make that lady offer me some of that good and pretty fried chicken. There was no place for colored people to eat on the trains in those days, especially down in Galilee (the South). Colored persons going North crammed their baskets full of everything but the kitchen stove.

Luckily the lady recognized me. She told me she knew Mayann and that she was going to Chicago too. We were both wondering about the big city, and we soon became very good friends. I lived and ate like a king during the whole trip.

Finally, when the conductor came through the train hollering "Chicago next stop" at the top of his voice, a funny feeling started running up and down my spine. The first thing I thought was: "I wonder if Papa Joe will be at the station waiting for me?" He expected me to come on the early morning train, but I had missed that because I had played at the funeral so as to have a little extra change when I hit Chicago.

I was all eyes looking out of the window when the train pulled into the station. Anybody watching me closely could have easily seen that I was a country boy. I certainly hoped Joe Oliver would be at the station. I was not particular about anyone else being there. All I wanted was to see Joe's face and everything would be rosy.

When the conductor hollered "All out for Chicago. Last stop" it looked like everybody rose from their seats at the same time. There was no sign of Joe on the platform, and when I climbed the long flight of stairs to the waiting room I still did not see any sign of him.

I had a million thoughts as I looked at all those people waiting for taxi cabs. It was eleven-thirty at night. All the colored people, including the lady with the chicken, who had come up from New Orleans, were getting into their cabs or relatives' cars. As they left they said good-bye and wished me good luck on my stay in Chicago. As I waved good-bye I thought to myself: "Huh. I don't think I am going to like this old town."

Suddenly I found myself standing all alone. And the longer I stood the more restless I got. I must have stood there about half an hour when a policeman came up to me. He had been watching me for a long time and he could see that I was a stranger in town and that I was looking worriedly for someone.

"Are you looking for someone?" he asked.

"Yes sir."

"Can I help you?"

"I came in from New Orleans, Louisiana," I said. "I am a cornet player, and I came up here to join Joe Oliver's Jazz Band."

He gave me a very pleasant smile.

"Oh," he said. "You are the young man who's to join King Oliver's band at the Lincoln Gardens."

"Yes sir," I said.

Then it struck me that he had just said *King* Oliver. In New Orleans it was just plain Joe Oliver.

I was so anxious to see him that that name was good enough for me. When I told the cop that King Oliver was supposed to meet me here he said:

[231]

"King Oliver was down here waiting for you to arrive on an earlier train, but you did not show up. He had to go to work, but he left word for us to look out for you if you came in on this train."

Then he waved to a taxi and told the driver: "Take this kid out to the place where King Oliver is playing." The driver put my bags into the cab and away we went toward the South Side.

As I opened the door to go into the Lincoln Gardens I could hear Joe's band swinging out on one of those good old Dixieland tunes. Believe me, I was really thrilled by the way they were playing. It was worth the price of my trip. But I was a little shaky about going inside. For a moment I wondered if I should. Then, too, I started wondering if I could hold my own with such a fine band. But I went in anyway, and the further in I got, the hotter the band got.

The Lincoln Gardens was located at Thirty-first and Cottage Grove Avenues. It had a beautiful front with a canopy that ran from the doorway to the street. The lobby seemed to be a block long, so long that I thought I was never going to reach the bandstand. The place was jammed with people and Joe and the boys did not see me until I was almost on the bandstand.

Then all hell seemed to break loose. All those guys jumped up at the same time saying: "Here he is! Here he is!" Joe Oliver took his left foot off the cuspidor on which he usually kept it when he was playing his cornet. He had a private cuspidor because he chewed tobacco all the time.

"Wait a minute, let me see him," Joe said to the boys. "Why I've not seen that little slow foot devil in years." He always used to call me "slow foot" whenever he visited me at the honky-tonk where I worked in New Orleans.

Joe began by asking me all kind of questions about what I had been doing since he and Jimmy Noone left New Orleans in 1918. He was tickled to death that I had gotten good enough to become a regular member of the well known Tuxedo Brass Band and that I had played on the boat.

"Gee, son, I'm really proud of you," Joe said. "You've been in some fast company since I last saw you."

The expression on his face proved that he was still in a little wonderment as to whether I was good enough to play with him and his boys. But he did not say so. All he said was:

"Have a seat, son, we're going to do our show. You might as well stick around and see what's happening because you start work tomorrow night."

"Yes sir," I said.

After the show was over Joe took me over to his house which was just around the corner from the Lincoln Gardens. Mrs. Stella Oliver, who had always been fond of me, was as glad to see me as I was to see her. With her was her daughter Ruby by another marriage.

[233]

They were a happy family and I became one of them.

Mrs. Stella said that I must have a meal with them, which was all right by me. The way Joe ate was right, and there were no formalities and stuff. She fed us a big dish of red beans and rice, a half loaf of bread and a bucket of good ice cold lemonade.

It was getting late and Mrs. Stella told Joe it was time to take me over to the room he had reserved for me in a boarding house at 3412 South Wabash Avenue, run by a friend of his named Filo. As we were going there in the taxi cab Joe told me that I would have a room and a private bath.

"Bath? Private bath? What's a private bath?" I asked.

"Listen you little slow foot sommitch," he said looking at me kind of funny, "don't be so damn dumb."

He had forgotten that he must have asked the same question when he first came up from New Orleans. In the neighborhood where we lived we never heard of such a thing as a bathtub, let alone a *private bath.* After Joe finished giving me hell about the question, I reminded him about the old days and how we used to take baths in the clothes washtub in the back yard, or else a foot tub. I can still remember when I used to take a bath in one of those tin tubs. In order to get real clean I would have to sit on the rim and wash myself from my neck to my middle. After that I would stand up and wash the rest of me. Papa Joe had to laugh when I told him about that.

Filo must have been waiting up for us because she came to the door the minute we rang the bell. She was a good-looking, middle-aged Creole gal. You could see the kindness in her face at once, and as soon as she spoke you felt relaxed.

"Is this my home boy?" she asked.

"Yep," Joe said, "this is old Dippermouth."

As soon as we came in Filo told me my room was upstairs and I could hardly wait to go up and witness that private bath of mine. However, I had to put that off because Filo and we sat around and talked ourselves silly about New Orleans as far back as any of us could remember. Filo had left New Orleans almost ten years before me, and she had come to Chicago even before Joe Oliver.

The next morning Filo fixed breakfast for me, and just like all Creole women she was a very good cook. After breakfast I went up and took a good hot bath in my private bathtub, and then I dressed to go out for a little stroll and see what the town looked like.

I did not know where I was going and I did not care much because everything looked so good. With all due respect to my home town every street was much nicer than the streets in New Orleans. In fact, there was no comparison.

When I reached home Filo had the big table all set up and waiting.

"Wash up," she said in her quiet voice, "and come

and get these good victuals." Filo had about every good Creole dish one could mention.

After the meal I went upstairs to shave, take a bath and have a good nap. Since I was a kid the old masters had taught me that plenty of sleep is essential for good music. A musician cannot play his best when he is tired and irritable.

When I woke up and was just about dressed Filo came into my room.

"Although you have had a hearty dinner," she said, "you have got a lot of blowing to do and you need some more to hold you up."

I did not argue about that. Downstairs she gave me a sandwich covered with pineapple and brown sugar. Boy, was it good! When I finished that sandwich I started out for the opening night at the Gardens.

I was wearing my old Roast Beef, which was what I called my ragged tuxedo. Of course I had it pressed and fixed up as good as possible so that no one would notice how old it was unless they looked real close and saw the patches here and there. Anyway I thought I looked real sharp.

At eight-thirty on the dot a cab pulled up in front of Filo's house. Filo had ordered it for she was as excited as I was and she wanted everything to go right for the night of my debut with the King. It is a funny thing about the music fame and show business, no matter how long you have been in the profession opening night always makes you feel as though little butterflies were running around in your stomach.

Mrs. Major, the white lady who owned the Gardens, and Red Bud, the colored manager, were the first people I ran into when I walked through the long lobby. Then I ran into King Jones, a short fellow with a loud voice you could hear over a block away when he acted as master of ceremonies. (He acted as though he was not a colored fellow, but his real bad English gave him away.)

When I reached the bandstand there was King Oliver and all his boys having a smoke before the first set and waiting for me to show up. The place was filling up with all the finest musicians from downtown including Louis Panico, the ace white trumpeter, and Isham Jones, who was the talk of the town in the same band.

I was thrilled when I took my place with that grand group of musicians: Johnny and Baby Dodds, Honore Dutrey, Bill Johnson, Lil Hardin and the master himself. It was good to be playing with Baby Dodds again; I was glad to learn he had stopped drinking excessively and had settled down to his music. He was still a wizard on the drums, and he certainly made me blow my horn that night when I heard him beat those sticks behind one of my hot choruses.

Johnny Dodds was a fine healthy boy and his variations were mellow and perfect. His hobby was watching the baseball scores, especially for the White Sox team. Johnny and I would buy the *Daily News*; he would take out the baseball scores and give me the rest of the paper.

Bill Johnson, the bass player, was the cat that interested me that first evening at the Gardens. He was one of the original Creole Jazz Band boys and one of the first to come North and make a musical hit. He had the features and even the voice of a white boy — an ofay, or Southern, white boy at that. His sense of humor was unlimited.

Dutrey had a wonderful sense of humor and a fine disposition to boot. How well I remembered how I used to follow him and Joe Oliver all day long during the street parades when I was a boy in New Orleans. When he was discharged from the Navy he went to Chicago to live and he had joined Joe Oliver a few weeks before I came to the city. He still played a beautiful horn, but he suffered badly from shortness of breath. Whenever he had a hard solo to play he would go to the back of the bandstand and spray his nose and throat. After that the hep cats would have to look out, for he would blow one whale of a trombone. How he did it was beyond me.

For a woman Lil Hardin was really wonderful, and she certainly surprised me that night with her four beats to a bar. It was startling to find a woman who had been valedictorian in her class at Fisk University fall in line and play such good jazz. She had gotten her training from Joe Oliver, Freddy Keppard,

Sugar Johnny, Lawrence Dewey, Tany Johnson and many other of the great pioneers from New Orleans. If she had not run into those top-notchers she would have probably married some big politician or maybe played the classics for a living. Later I found that Lil was doubling after hours at the Idleweise Gardens. I wondered how she was ever able to get any sleep. I knew those New Orleans cats could take it all right, but it was a tough pull for a woman.

When we cracked down on the first note that night at the Lincoln Gardens I knew that things would go well for me. When Papa Joe began to blow that horn of his it felt right like old times. The first number went over so well that we had to take an encore. It was then that Joe and I developed a little system for the duet breaks. We did not have to write them down. I was so wrapped up in him and lived so closely to his music that I could follow his lead in a split second. No one could understand how we did it, but it was easy for us and we kept it up the whole evening.

I did not take a solo until the evening was almost over. I did not try to go ahead of Papa Joe because I felt that any glory that came to me must go to him. He could blow enough horn for both of us. I was playing second to his lead, and I never dreamed of trying to steal the show or any of that silly rot.

Every number on opening night was a gassuh. A special hit was a piece called *Eccentric* in which Joe took a lot of breaks. First he would take a four bar break, then the band would play. Then he would take another four bar break. Finally at the very last chorus Joe and Bill Johnson would do a sort of musical act. Joe would make his horn sound like a baby crying, and Bill Johnson would make his horn sound as though it was a nurse calming the baby in a high voice. While Joe's horn was crying, Bill Johnson's horn would interrupt on that high note as though to say, "Don't cry, little baby." Finally this musical horseplay broke up in a wild squabble between nurse and child, and the number would bring down the house with laughter and applause.

After the floor show was over we went into some dance tunes, and the crowd yelled, "Let the youngster blow!" That meant me. Joe was wonderful and he gladly let me play my rendition of the blues. That was heaven.

Papa Joe was so elated that he played half an hour over time. The boys from downtown stayed until the last note was played and they came backstage and talked to us while we packed our instruments. They congratulated Joe on his music and for sending to New Orleans to get me. I was so happy I did not know what to do.

I had hit the big time. I was up North with the greats. I was playing with my idol, the King, Joe Oliver. My boyhood dream had come true at last.